Advanced Freelancing

Contents

Contents	2
Starting out	8
What is an advanced freelancer?	9
Why freelancing is not for you	10
What to include in your freelance portfolio	14
How to create a portfolio with no previous work	16
3 rules for branding your freelance business	18
How to pick your freelancing niche	20
Why all freelancers should write a manifesto	22
How to write the perfect freelance case study	23
Selling	25
Understanding Sales versus Marketing	26
A sales process for advanced freelancers	29
9 sales tips for freelancers	31
5 things freelance clients want to know	33
Negotiation for freelancers	35
How to cold email a freelance lead	37
Cold Calling for freelancers	39
One sure fire way to win a freelance job	40

How much should a freelancer charge?	42
Payment methods for freelancers	44
Ways you will not get paid for your work	46
How freelancers can make sure they get paid	49
Why freelancers shouldn't use bidding websites	51
Why freelancers shouldn't use contest websites	53
8 red flags to avoid bad freelance clients	54

Working   56

How to handle these 6 types of freelance clients	57
Why customer service should be a priority	60
How to provide exceptional customer service	61
Where should you work?	63
What to do when you have no freelance work	65
Holidays for freelancers	67
Budgeting for freelancers	70

Growing   74

Turn your freelance project into a long-term client	75
Stand out from the crowd on job sites	76
How delegating tasks can improve your workflow	79
6 ways to optimise sales conversion for freelancer	81
How to win freelance work without proposals	83
How client testimonials will help	85
How you can double your freelance income overnight	88

Starting out

What is an advanced freelancer?

Advanced freelancers are different to your typical freelancer in a few important ways. They are reliable when they take work on. They're consistent in their approach. They do their particular service or craft as a full-time job and enjoy it. And they're aspiring to create a reputation or brand to help grow their business in the future. But if you were to sum it up in one sentence; they reduce the risk for their customers.

That's not to say that someone freelancing part-time, or moonlighting is any worse at their job. But there are legitimate concerns with hiring people that aren't in it for the long-haul. As an advanced freelancer, you owe it to yourself to make sure it's clear you're not like the rest. And you will win more work if this is clear to your customers.

Why is it important?

A potential customer wants to complete their project without any drama, such as you disappearing half way through, or not being able to do what you claim. They have an expectation of the outcome and try to find the most likely person to get them there. Your primary job is to minimise all the things that they think could go wrong. And there are signals you can give out that help do that.

Here are a few different ways I used to differentiate myself as an advanced freelancer:

- Register a company and use an accountant & lawyer
- Use a custom domain name for your website and email
- State your bookable hours, and your available hours
- Write in-depth case studies around the project goals and include references/testimonials.
- Write and talk about your values and strengths
- Be clear about what you won't or can't do
- Set expectations early about how the work will be carried out

If you think some of these are obvious, then you're likely to be an advanced freelancer, or on your way there. But it's surprising how many freelancers don't do these things.

Be aware that these things do not ensure you'll be successful, if by success you mean more work, with less effort. Successful freelancers use this as a foundation to win more work.

Why freelancing is not for you (and how you can make it work)

The amount of people who choose to freelance is on the rise and how we seek employment are changing. PeoplePerHour founder Xenios Thrasyvoulou has said that "we predict by 2020, 50% of the workforce will be self-employed and contributing more than £51 billion to the UK economy" and that the current model of employment is becoming "obsolete". On the surface, the flexibility and diversity that a career in freelancing provides, appears to make it the perfect mode of acquiring income.

However, there is another side. Alessandro Nivola, actor and producer has stated that "anybody who is in freelance work, especially artistically, knows that it comes with all the insecurity and the ups and downs". Not everyone has a positive experience.
A labour source survey in 2016 discovered that the distribution of self-employed income is on average £240 per week, which is much lower than the average £400 employees receive. This is in part because many freelancers don't earn enough to make freelancing their

full-time occupation. Instead, they use it as a part-time job to supplement their income. Many others abandon it altogether in favour of the security that employment brings.

So what factors contribute towards a negative experience of freelancing, and how can these problems be solved to make it work for you?

Lack of stability

Working for yourself means that you don't have the structure of a business to look after you and rely on. The volume of work can hugely fluctuate, as it depends on a variety of unstable factors such as unreliable clients, personal experience levels or the amount of work available.

Solutions:
Create a retainer agreement with an agency: These are designed to provide regular monthly payments to a freelancer to secure their availability for work in that amount of time.
You can review articles such as https://doubleyourfreelancing.com/freelancers-guide-cli

ent-retainer-agreements/ to help you in your understanding of this area.

Sign up for job notifications: If you are searching for a steadier income, job advertising sites often offer long-term, remote working projects that are contracted for security.

Sign up to multiple platforms: Expanding your reach through the use of multiple different websites can provide a larger volume of work.

Limited clientele

Building up your portfolio and reputation is one of the hardest challenges that a freelancer has to face, particularly at the beginning of their career. When applying for work, if there is someone with more experience and a more extensive portfolio, they have a much greater chance of securing the contract. Many freelancers feel as though they need to work for free or for incredibly low pay in order to make any later successes. However this does not have to be the case.

Solutions:
Persevere: For the first few months of any freelancing career it will take time to build up your reputation, portfolio and endorsements. Persevering through this

stage is worth it, because the work is likely to pick up pace later.

Build your online portfolio: Develop a collection of your work and display it through your own website or blog, using social media to increase the traffic you receive. You can also increase your portfolio through guest posting on websites.

Time management

Usually, when working within an organisation, employees are given standardised working hours and a set amount of work. There are well-managed expectations and other people who can assist you, contribute to the work and pick up the slack. However, working alone on large or multiple projects can mean long and unsociable hours of work. This can cause a great deal of stress if you are over-ambitious with the amount of time you have.

Solutions:
Standardise your working hours and create boundaries. If your work begins to creep beyond your designated hours, it shows that you have taken on too much.
Manage client expectations. Facilitating open communication about work progress and setting a time frame with clients can reduce the pressure.

Complete work before moving on: Having a to-do list and completing one task at a time in manageable chunks will reduce the pressure of your overall workload.

Administration tasks

As a freelancer, there is a lot more work involved than simply completing projects and liaising with clients. All the administration tasks such as taxes, invoices and finances are your responsibility and it may not be everybody's field of expertise.

Solutions:
Project management tools: There are many available applications that can help you manage your finances. Websites such as GnuCash and Buddi are good beginners' tools for organising this aspect of a business.
Keep up to date with invoices: This includes ensuring that your invoices are being paid in a timely fashion. Having a payment discussion with a client or sending a reminder email are both important means of making sure you are up to date. Also completing invoices quickly means they don't pile up.

Procrastination and poor motivation

As a freelancer, there isn't anybody telling you how to work, when to work or how hard to work. This means that all work is dependant on good levels of motivation and willpower. If these are skills that you lack, freelancing offers very few incentives to get you working consistently.

Solutions:
Choose projects of interest: When applying for pieces of work, it is not always possible to choose something that is exactly within your niche. However, choosing projects that interest and excite you can help maintain levels of motivation for a project.
Well defined targets: Setting yourself achievable targets ensures that you have something manageable to aim for. For example, how many pieces of work you would like to complete in a week

Working alone

In comparison with the sociable atmosphere of an office, freelancing can promote unhealthy working habits, such as staying isolated for extended periods of time. The convenience of online communication means that many work-related conversations will happen over a messaging service and much of the work is completed independently. Working alone means that you must have an incredibly motivated attitude towards your work.

Solutions:
Look into co-working spaces: Websites such as www.coworker.com or www.wework.com can be used to find a shared office space in which to work.
Work in a public space: Moving your work out of your house into a coffee shop or a library can increase the socialisation you experience whilst you are working and also gives you the chance to work away from the house.
Make time in your schedule for friends and family: With long and unsociable working hours, it can be easy to prioritise work over family and friends. Try to make time in the structure of your day to see other people, or phone loved ones.

Holiday and sick pay

When employed by a company, statutory sick pay is a mandatory provision and is the minimum amount you can be paid if you're off sick. When a contract is signed at a place of employment, usually holiday pay will be a feature of the agreement.

As a self-employed worker, not receiving sick or holiday pay is a problem that has to be managed carefully. Freelancers have financial autonomy and when they cannot fulfil their work obligations, they are unable to get paid.

Solutions:
Retainer agreements: As mentioned previously, a retainer agreement can be incredibly productive as it guarantees a set amount of income each month.
Upfront payment jobs: Larger projects usually require either a deposit or an upfront payment in order to complete them. If you know there is a month in which you are taking a holiday, a job in which you are given an initial payment can give you the security of some income for the month.
Track your spending and save: Making sure you keep an excellent track of your finances is crucial to limit the damage that sickness can cause to your business.

There are aspects of every career or job that are negative, but almost always there is a solution. Freelancing has high risks as a career choice, but the enjoyment and fulfilment that can be gained (for many) is worth the extra measures needed to make it a success.

What to include in your freelance portfolio (except for the obvious)

1. Your name, location and contact details.
2. Examples of your past work.

It's pretty clear that most freelancers know what to put in their portfolio. But what they don't know is that you can make it much easier to win work if they go further than the average freelancer.

Stories

Case studies are non-fictional stories about what you were hired to do, what challenges you faced, and what outcome you produced. Clients care about the story because it gives them some context about what you do and what you can do for them. So case studies aren't just pictures, text or code. They're insight into how you work.

Whilst writing a case study, imagine you're writing it for the 100 other similar companies that can benefit from your services. What do they want to know? Usually it's a simple as solving a problem. But you should go into the specifics of why your solution solves their problems in the best way for their industry or product.

Here's a really short example that takes you through a common request and outcome that I used to run into:

SuchAndSuch Ltd. approached me to redesign their home page. We talked about what their goals were, and it turned out that sales had been dropping ever since a competitor had been outspending them on Adwords. I proposed that instead of re-designing their homepage, we try to do something to increase referral traffic. They were under a lot of pressure, and this solution would yield results quicker than increasing organic traffic. And obviously do much more for them than a homepage redesign would. Their product was very novel and easily shared, so I designed the UX flow for a referrals system. It rewarded anyone that shared their favourite products with their friends with a discount. This amounted to the equivalent that the client was spending to acquire a customer. It launched 4 weeks later when we emailed every past customer letting them know about the new offer. In the first 4 weeks after launch, they had cut their ad spend by 25% and increased organic traffic by 300%. Their sales revenue also increased 15% for the month following the launch.

It addresses why I was hired, how I identified their deepest problems and helped fix them. It tells people how fast I fixed the problem and how I worked out how to make it affordable for their business.

What if there aren't any spectacular results? As long as you address the clients goals and try to reach them, it's a success. Most of the work we do is experimental and iterative. People are smart enough to realise you can't deliver amazing results in every situation — the key thing is how you worked with them and what state you left them in.

Most case studies I read on freelancers portfolios go as far as telling me the client name and services that were carried out. What clients really want to know is — what is it like to work with you.

Values

Knowing what type of freelancer you are and what you stand for goes a long way to convincing someone to hire you. I've already written about why you should write a manifesto. The key thing to remember is that customers buy from people they feel most similar too (this is branding), so you can attract the right kind of clients by writing about your own values.

Pricing

An idea of price along with your services helps you attract the type of work you need. Most freelancers are concerned with turning off clients that you may still be able to help. Pricing is tricky. You should try displaying prices within a range. Add prices to your case studies to give people an idea of how much you cost in specific scenarios.

Knowledge

Writing about what you've learnt is the best signal to a potential customer that you know what you're doing. Sharing what you know shows confidence in what you do. You should aim to write a couple of articles on things you've tried and learnt from, for every project you're involved in.

Action

Make it easy to start working with you. There should be a call to action with every piece of your portfolio. The easier it is to start working with you, the more likely you are to receive inbound leads from potential customers.

How to create a portfolio with no previous work

Research suggests that only 35% of freelancers have an online portfolio for their work. However, 64% of freelancers say that they use the internet to find work. Whether online or offline, a portfolio can be an incredibly powerful tool to help demonstrate how valuable you can be to a client and why they should hire you. A portfolio reflects your experience, expertise, creativity, knowledge and skill. Furthermore, it showcases all of these attributes through proven case studies and the tangible results you achieve.

However, when you are starting out as a freelancer, you are unlikely to have any previous work to include if your portfolio. So, how can you create a powerful portfolio that wins clients with no prior work? Here are just some of the ways you can build up a portfolio from scratch.

Begin with your bio

Your biography should help to introduce you and your portfolio to your client. Consider your bio as the 'about us' page of a website; in fact, your portfolio may even be a website, depending on your industry. The bio should be a quick overview of who you are, what you do and the critical skills, experience and qualifications you have.

It can be challenging to write about yourself in your bio and give off the ideal perception. With this in mind, it can help to get your friends and family to read your bio and state three adjectives that they think of when they read it. For example, goal-getting, creative and analytical. These adjectives should be the same as the message you want to portray. If they are misaligned, your bio may need a review.

Remember, it is wise to keep your bio short and sweet. Clients are more likely to focus on the examples in your portfolio and your proven abilities, more than what you say you do.

Add your manifesto

A manifesto explains who you are as a freelancer. It doesn't demonstrate your work. Instead, it states who you are as a freelancer. Consider your manifesto as declaring your values. This way, you can attract like-minded clients who share your values. This not only helps you to find clients but helps you to attract the right clients. When you share similar values to your clients, you are far more likely to build a healthy and positive working relationship.

Being on the same page as your clients can really help to secure long-term relationships, so don't be afraid to be honest in your manifesto. You have the chance to talk about your style, your focus and niche, your expertise, and how you operate as a person. For example, if you donate a certain amount of profits to a charity, your manifesto is a great place to share this information and explain exactly what is important to you as a freelancer.

A skills profile

You don't need to have had paying clients to build up a selection of skills. You may have built up skills from academic projects, online courses, self-studying, volunteering or any other format. However, make sure that these skills are relevant to your portfolio and freelance business. There is no point listing skills that you don't want to utilise as a freelancer.

There are lots of ways you can document your skills in your portfolio, from including certificates, listing skills or perhaps including sample pieces of work for each talent. If you do include sample work, just add a note to make it clear that these are examples and not work that a client has paid for.

Example pieces

Just because you haven't had paying clients, doesn't mean you cannot exercise your skills in creating example work. You may find it is beneficial to generate example pieces for your own business that you can utilise elsewhere as a freelancer. For example, web designers can demonstrate their portfolio by creating a stunning online portfolio website. Alternatively, designers can come up with a concept for their own business needs.

Freelancers may also find it beneficial to seek out briefs from other companies even if the company didn't hire them. It can also help to demonstrate initiative if you spot an issue that a company has and then creating example pieces of work of how you would fix it. Many businesses like freelancers who are willing to use their initiative and go beyond the brief to find the root cause of an issue and, then, offer suggestions of how to improve it.

Again, it is crucial to add a note to any examples you create that these are purely sample pieces and not paid pieces of work.

Social media and contact information

If you use social media to showcase your talents, then make sure these are easy to find in your portfolio. This means clients can explore your skills further if they want further information. It is wise only to have industry-specific or 'business' social media accounts. If your personal social media accounts may not show you in the best light, leave them out. Your social media accounts should help not hinder your business as a freelancer.

When posting content on your social media, make sure that it demonstrates a keen interest in the industry and is relevant to your work. Before posting to the world, ask yourself; 'Am I happy for clients to see this?'

Finally, after wowing clients with your portfolio, you need to make it incredibly easy for clients to contact you. Keep your contact information up to date on your portfolio and easily visible so clients know exactly how they can get in touch to discuss their next project.

3 rules for branding your freelance business

A brand isn't something you create or control, but you can try and shape it with style, imagery and succinct messages (tag-lines). A brand is the perception of your company before they've spoken to you. And it's important for a freelancer, because growing your business relies on people recommending you to others that have no idea who you are.

Branding usually includes a logo, colours e.t.c., but for a freelancer, these are the parts that rarely matter. What matters is how people speak about you to others, and you can give them the tools to do that to your benefit.

A good brand for a freelancer is actually just the way you carry out your business. Knowing your values, and following through with them is the way you should be building your brand.

Here's the 3 rules to help you think differently about it…

1. No logo

You should concentrate on the parts of your brand that will be shared and recognised by others. Most of your inbound leads should come from word of mouth referrals by other people and current customers. These people will not be sharing your logo. At most they will share your photo, but primarily they'll be describing the reasons to work with you. Think about what those reasons should be. After you've worked with a customer, as well as following up with more ways you can help out you should also be asking for referrals. And giving them good reasons why they should do it.

2. No bullshit

First of all, don't name your company anything other than your name. Even if you have wider aspirations, for a good long while you're going to be building the company off your own back. Being honest about your size and concentrating on personal relationships will give you more credibility. Faking it until you make it might work for some people, but it's much easier to be honest. Made up company names don't help with your sales or your client relationships. It's much more attractive to be dealing with you on a personal level than having some fake abstraction designed to make me think you're bigger than you are.

3. Over-deliver

The number one reason people refer services is because they were blown away by what they expected versus what they got. And the key thing to remember is that they have to be blown away, not just happy. Go beyond the things in your proposal and do something unexpected and valuable. Start-ups and marketers sometimes call this the a-ha! moment in a product on-boarding cycle. In my experience, this isn't just delivering great work — that should be, and usually is expected. Every-time I went further than just delivering great work, it helped me to grow my own business. This can be as simple as providing insight into another area of their business, or identifying and solving a different problem for them before they know it.

Put simply, branding isn't what most people think it is. And for freelancers, it's none of the obvious stuff like a logo or a colour palette. It's the way your customers describe you to others. And putting some effort into thinking about this gives your customers a reason to not just describe your brand, but to love it enough to share it.

How to pick your freelancing niche

A freelance niche refers to a small segment of the total market that buys freelance services. This can be defined as a "horizontal" segment, usually focused on a particular service, like "Copywriting". And a "vertical" segment, focused on a particular sector of an industry, like online retail. Ignore broad service segments (horizontal), because nobody seeks out services. They want to solve their problems. Instead, I'll try to convince you to focus on the problems of a specific industry (vertical). The goal is to spend the least amount of time winning work, and more time billing.

Problem based selling

Sell solutions to a painful problem, with proof of results in a particular industry, and you will win work with ease.

Clients don't shop around for services, like content marketing or conversion optimisation. They seek out the best person to solve a particular problem, like "More sales for my online shoe shop", or "More fans of my sports team". They will also have concerns about skills not being transferable between industries. For an easier sell, you should show solid examples and results from working for other businesses in the same industry.

So the way to think about your niche is in 2 parts:
What problem am I solving?
Who am I solving it for?

And then get specific enough to make yourself uncomfortable. Really specific. You're talking to one business, whilst excluding the rest of them. This works because most successful businesses have many competitors. If you're targeting one particular type of business, you're actually able to talk to many of them the same way.

A bad example that I see often, would be: "Re-designs for Small Business"

A better, but still not specific enough example would be "Conversion optimisation for online retailers".

A good example would be: "Increased sales for online sport retailers."

In the good example, we've picked the biggest problem we can think of for a particular type of customer in a specific industry. And that type of customer is easy to find. Google "buy sports equipment online" and you'll have many businesses to talk to. Most importantly, you've made it easy to show these customers why they should hire you to solve this problem. One case study of your skills applied to this problem in this industry should put you way ahead of any other freelancer.

Now we've decided on online sports retailers, how do we know we can build a business around them? We need to test out the size of the market, and how repeatable our sales could be.

Testing your niche

Now you're convinced that problem based selling is easier than service based selling. But how do you know which businesses have the most pain from this problem?

1. Pick an industry you have experience in, e.g. Team Sports and pair it with a painful problem for this industry, e.g. Community building

2. Find out how to repeatedly contact and pitch your experience to those customers. Trying giving them free advice related to solving this problem.

3. Track your conversion rate from pitch to winning work, aim for 10%. If you get over 10%, you're onto something.

This will require a lot of research and experimentation, but it's worth doing to make sure you aren't missing better opportunities. I recommend re-doing this every 3–6 months even if you are comfortable, because if the market shifts you don't want to be left behind.

Specialists win customers, generalists keep them

Once you've won a customer based on solving a specific problem for them, there are many ways you can solve that problem. This will help you scale your freelance business efficiently — by up-selling to existing customers, as well as finding new ones. Show you can solve their problems, and there will always be work for you to do.

Remember the goal

The less time you spend finding and selling to potential customers, the more time you will have to bill them. Companies in the same industry talk to each other, share contacts and emulate their competitors. You should be able to build recognition for your work in a single industry, and eventually start expanding into others.

Why all freelancers should write a manifesto

Your manifesto sets out the values in which you do your work. It includes things you don't stand for as much as things you do. It's important because people like to buy from people with similar values. When you make your values clear, it's easier to find customers that agree with you, and that you'll have a good working relationship with.

Writing a manifesto gives you the chance to think about why you are a freelancer and what kind of difference you want to make. It can all get a bit cliche, but it's important to have an external reason to stay motivated to do what you do. Setting out your values also sets you apart from people that don't take their vocation as seriously. That's a good thing.

What do you value?

So how do you start to write a manifesto? Think about the successful agencies and freelancers that exist today. They each have a particular angle, that gets them a specific type of client. Sometimes that's by design and sometimes it's luck. Getting lucky is great, but I'd prefer to think about and plan the type of work I want to do, rather than getting lucky. Here are some questions you can think about to get you started...

Do you strive for awards and publicity or stay private and exclusive?
Do you try to help as many people as possible or focus on one single project at a time?
Are you an enterprise supplier or an entrepreneur's best friend?
Do you use and give back to open source or prefer custom written software?Do you donate some percentage of profits to a specific charity?
Is your focus on a particular industry? Why?
Are you a minimalist or creatively vibrant?

The best way to think about what you value is to identify problems you see in how other companies conduct their business. The best kind of businesses start because they find a problem with how something is currently done.

A manifesto can be a living document that you change and update as your business grows and your experience increases. Even if you have very little experience, there's no excuse not to think about the type of work you want to do in the future.

How to write the perfect freelance case study

Not all case studies are created equally. Most are pretty shit actually. For freelancers that aren't professional writers it can be quite daunting or difficult to see the benefits. The truth is, nobody really cares about pictures of the end result without knowing what went into it. Without any context it's pretty useless. Most end-products are unique to a client's business and their specific goals. What prospective clients care about is your approach.

You should aim to cover the 3 stages of your approach:

1. Identify the problem

Your client will usually approach you with a task that needs completing. That's not really what you're there for though, right? Explain how you took their initial enquiry and worked backwards to find out what problems they're trying to solve. This might include client questionnaires or interviews, and maybe a face to face meeting. Explain your process for finding the problem shows your experience and interest in the companies you work for.

2. Understand the problem

Where does the problem fit into the business? Is it going to kill the company or is it just decoration? How important is it to the company and what have they tried already? Showing that you understand problems in the context of the business assures potential clients that you are reactive to their needs rather than knocking out generic services for everyone.

3. Solve the problem

What are the business goals and how are you going to reach them? What would success look like and what happens if it fails? How did you get stakeholders sign off? This is where all your work pays off, so try to quantify what it did for the business and include testimonials about how they felt once you'd completed the work.

3 things to quantify in your case study:
How long it took
How much it cost
What were the results

These 3 bits of key information should be spelled out clearly. For example: "Revenue increased 20%" or "Sign up conversion went from 1% to 6%".

So how do you begin writing one? Before writing case studies you should know exactly what industry and services you're targeting. If you have a track record working for a particular industry or providing a specific service, you should write case studies geared towards that. If you're looking to move into a new industry or test out new services, it's a good idea to get a few projects done for less than your typical price just to have case studies to sell it properly.

You should aim to have a case study for every type of service you offer, and in every type of industry you work in. For a web developer this might be, creating an app from scratch (from idea to execution) and refactoring an existing app (implementing tests and making them pass).

Case studies should also include challenges that you faced. Don't exclude negative aspects of the project unless you handled them badly! Challenges are to be expected, and if your case study doesn't have any then I'd be suspicious.

Selling

Understanding Sales versus Marketing

In boardrooms around the globe the term 'sales and marketing' are often whispered in one breath, like they are synonymous, two sides of the same coin, with many businesses having teams whose responsibility is to execute on both fronts.

It is undeniable that sales and marketing are closely linked. So much so that there are often blurred lines as to where one finishes and other starts. However, they should certainly be understood and applied as separate entities.

This is especially true when it comes to growing your freelance business. By understanding the difference between sales and marketing, you will be able to increase effectiveness by applying them in the right way.

What is sales?

Before we can go on to explain how the two can work together we must first clearly define what we mean by each. Although the term 'sales' can mean a number of different things, in the context of sales and marketing...

"Selling is any transaction in which money is exchanged for a good or service. During a sales negotiation, the seller attempts to convince or 'sell' the buyer on the benefits of their offer. [...] Put simply, selling is the act of persuading." – HubSpot

So, selling is the act of making a sale. No surprise there. But more specifically selling is the point at which the buyer is close to making a buying decision. Selling is usually a direct human to human act.

In terms of actions. Undertaking sales includes making calls to the customer, emailing a customer directly, and meeting with the customer face to face.

What is marketing?

In contrast, marketing is everything that leads up and surrounds sales activity...

"Marketing is the process of getting people interested in your company's product or service. This happens through market research, analysis, and understanding your ideal customer's interests. Marketing pertains to all aspects of a business, including product development, distribution methods, sales, and advertising." – HubSpot

From this definition, we can see that marketing is used to 'prime' potential customers ready to make a sale. Marketing tends to be undertaken with a longer-term view than sales, slowly building your business reputation. This means if you have marketed yourself correctly, when you pick up the phone to make a sales call the customer will already know who you are, what you do and will have trust in you.

Marketing activities span wide and far. Some examples include search engine optimisation, content marketing, social media, and print ads.

Getting the connection right

So, we now know what we mean by marketing and how that differs from sales. But how do they work in relation to each other? Here we turn our attention away from the dedicated purpose and actions within sales and marketing. We instead focus on the customer journey from a relative unknown (gaining awareness) to becoming a customer (making a purchase).

Marketing clearly fits into the awareness stage and sales clearly into the purchase stage. The middle stages show the relationship between two with interest, consideration, intent and evaluation all calling upon both skills in some way.

But what does this mean? Practically it shows us that sales and marketing, although separate, rely on each other in order to achieve success.

In the freelancer space, we often see individuals focusing on using just one. For example, a copywriter may primarily use content marketing in an attempt to drive sales of their services. On the flip side, a web developer may rely solely on their personal network to drive sales.

This is common primarily due to capacity. With freelancers often opting for the option that best suits their skills or provides the best returns.

This approach is far from wrong. But it is unlikely to return the best results, at least from a long term point of view. Relying solely on one marketing or sales technique leaves you vulnerable to changes in the market.

When is one better than the other?

So, the best long term strategy for freelancers is to create a mix of marketing and sales activities that create a reliable stream of jobs. However, there are times when a freelancer should lean more heavily on one than the other.

Marketing is at its most beneficial when used with the future in mind. Most marketing activities are unlikely to bring you a sale the day you execute them. For example, a perfectly written blog post (or series of blog posts) will help you build more, relevant search engine traffic to your site over time.

Sales, on the other hand, is most likely to drive more immediate action. Although at a level, sales should always be happening. This direct approach to winning work can be leaned on more during quiet periods. This is especially true as sales can be a time-consuming activity, which can be ramped up when other paid work is ticking over at a lower level.

Getting the job done

We have already discussed how sales and marketing can be time-consuming. This is a bigger issue for freelancers than it is for bigger businesses as your time is a rare and precious commodity.

Luckily, smart planning, technology and other freelancers can help you maintain the needed level of sales and marketing activity without the need to work every hour in the day.

Planning

Planning is the single most important thing you can do when looking to grow your freelance business with sales and marketing. This will save you a vast amount of time and allow you to quickly and easily leverage the below methods to increase your activity without detracting from your personal or paid time.

We could go deep into detail on how to create a complex and overarching marketing plan. However, for the busy freelancers, your marketing plan can follow just three simple steps:

Set your objectives (what do you want to achieve?)
Decide how you will reach those objectives (which sales and marketing techniques will you use?)
Note down how you will measure success.

Automation

When you are selling yourself (a freelancer) never underestimate the power of authenticity.
With this warning in mind, we can still use automation to help increase our sales and marketing activities.
However, these should never be used in a way which can make you seem in-human or as spam.

Good automation tools you may use for marketing include social media scheduling (Hootsuite), email marketing (MailChimp) and even chatbots to help customers find the right solution for them.

Outsourcing

Other marketing methods and the majority of sales techniques can be outsourced to other freelancers or businesses. For example, you may consider outsourcing blog writing, website writing, marketing campaigns, and direct sales.

A sales process for advanced freelancers

Like any entrepreneur, advanced freelancers should be working on their business, as well as in it. The sales process is the first thing I worked on, and optimised, because of the importance of it. This guide will take you through finding leads, discussing the project and closing the deal. Sales for an advanced freelancer should take up at least 20% of your time during engagements. And 100% of your time in a dry spell.

Lead generation

The most tedious and least rewarding part of your job is going to be lead generation. This is finding potential customers for your services.

Start with the problem you're trying to solve. Who has this problem? How are they solving it right now? Who feels the most pain from it? Figure out who they might be, where they are and how you're going to reach them. Common types of customers for web freelancers are:
Small, local businesses
Entrepreneurs starting up

Other freelancers and agencies
Non-profit organisations

I made this easy for myself. I kept a list of job boards, websites, communities, and social media searches. These sites had people posting their projects and asking for freelance help. This was a quicker way to get their contact details and partially qualify them.

You can make it easy to begin with too, by talking to everyone in your network. Talk to people who you think might need your help. And if they don't, ask them if they know someone who is. You'll find it much easier to qualify and close deals with people this way to begin with.

Qualifying leads

So you have a bunch of emails or phone numbers. You now need to reduce those down to people that actually need your help.

You're aiming to send out a lot of messages, or make a lot of phone calls. Expect to lose around 70% of your leads to begin with, which means for every 10 messages you send, only 1–3 will reply. For every 10 of those, around 1–3 will show interest in working with you. That means you need to send around 100 cold emails or make 100 cold calls to qualify 20–30 people, and win 1–3 projects. This is where most freelancers fail, because they don't put in enough effort.

Most freelancers will jump right into pitching their services and how great they are. This is wrong. Don't do that. The goal here is to find out if they have the problems you solve in the first place. If they don't, who cares how great you and your solutions are?

Send an email or phone them and ask one simple question, Do you have this problem I'm trying to solve? If "No", rephrase the question or give up, you decide. If you get a "Yes", then talk to them about it. How do they solve it right now? How painful is it? And always do this in person or over a phone call. It's impossible to let the conversation flow over email.

Another important step here is to always follow up, if you don't hear back after a day or two. Following up is like rocket fuel for your conversion rate.

The more you talk to people who you think would benefit from your services, the more you'll learn about who to target and why. You don't need to be selling right now, you need to be listening. However, I would ask them how much they could spend to solve this issue.

If you've understood their problem and think you can help, it's time to move on. But what happens next? Well, you decide. The theme throughout this process is that you do all the work, so they don't have to. At this point, I would tell them I'd like to help, and schedule another call. On that call, we'll go through a proposal that attempts to solve their problem. And at the end of that call, I would tell them when I'd like to get started.

Getting started

If it's easy to get started, they're more likely to do it. When breaking up the work in milestones, make the first one less than a week. If I hire someone new, I want to see progress so I can judge whether we're on the right path or not.

The logistics of getting started are simple. You should always sign a contract that outlines the work to be done, how it will be done and when it will be delivered. But don't be fooled into thinking this is it. To confirm the work, take a small deposit as well. Make sure they understand the work involved, as false expectations cause problems in the future.

9 sales tips for freelancers

Over the last 7 years of selling freelance services, I've picked up on a few things that repeat themselves. If you apply any of them, you'll hopefully avoid learning a lesson the hard way.

Embed yourself in their business

Once a customer shows interest in working with you, spend time learning about their business. Not only will this give you an edge in selling, it will make you a better freelancer. Put together a proposal after asking a lot of questions and doing your research. Tailor your solution to their circumstance, industry, and location. Focus on adding as much value as possible, even if it's outside your remit.

Say No

Practice it, and get used to it. If you have a gut feeling, go with it. There are plenty more good clients out there and if one is giving you a dodgy feeling about payment terms or project scope, drop them.

Don't cut costs

It's tempting to win work by being cheaper. But your motivation will decrease and the quality of work will go down. Charge the amount that makes you feel happy and confident about doing the work. If they can't afford it then decrease the scope of the work.

Run the numbers

Try and talk to A LOT of people. Having a wide funnel helps you figure out who your ideal client is, what their problems are and how best to serve them. Once you start learning more about your customers, your conversion rate will improve. I used to send out 1–5 initial messages every day, resulting in about a 30% conversion rate to initial phone call and just a 3% conversion to a closed deal.

Stop selling, start listening

Ask questions and find out as much as possible about the customer, their business, and their problems. Don't sell preconceived solutions to problems that don't exist. Basically, don't assume you know it all.

Act fast

Move the process along as quickly as you can. This will push better clients to the top of your list and discard ones who aren't serious. If a problem is worth solving, it's worth solving today.

Always think long term

Under promise and over deliver is a cliche, but it works if your goal is to keep customers coming back. Selling your time is awful for scaling, but building a brand can help you scale further than you think.

Do all the work

Don't make your customers think. Don't leave it to them to follow up with you or suggest the next step. Always have a plan and always keep moving. If you lose a customer because they didn't get around to doing something, you should have done it for them.

Ask for the sale

Rarely do people pay you for things without you asking first. Closing more deals could be as simple as asking for them. For example, asking when a customer wants to get started is weak. Telling them you want to get started tomorrow and asking for a deposit is better.

5 things freelance clients want to know

Selling your services as a freelancer is probably not the way you want to spend your time. But if you want to do good work you must be good at selling yourself too. It doesn't have to be difficult, if you know what your customers want.

Solid examples of relevant experience

Portfolios are a good start, but you need to explain where your experience came from. In-depth case studies of past work are essential. They're great for demonstrating what you do, how you do it, and if it works for your customers. You should also include testimonials and statistics where they're relevant.

Clients reduce their risk by finding people with experience relevant to their needs. That includes offering the right services, but also extends to skills, technology used and industry worked in. The best way to close bigger deals is to win smaller, similar work, first. And then detail every result you achieved, and how you did it.

Understanding their business goals

Retaining customers as a freelancer will help you grow faster. Adding more value than you're hired for is a great way to do that. I used to work with start-ups only, and I would (and still do) immerse myself in their industry, so that I knew what they knew. That meant we shared the same reference points when talking about particular strategies and goals.

Being genuinely interested in a clients business is the best way to convince them to hire you. And it's also essential for enjoying the work you do. Long term, it helps you build a track record in a particular industry, which means you can start to offer more insight to your customers.

How much is it going to cost

Freelance services are often assumed to have predictable costs. Unfortunately there is no market price list. The answer is, it depends.

That doesn't mean you can be vague and expect them to hire you anyway. If you're asked "How much?", you should do you best to find out as soon as possible. This means asking questions about their goals and working out the scope of the work involved. When I did this for my customers, I would break it down into the first thing I could do in less than 1 week, that gets them on the right path.

You should always ask for a budget, but if you don't get an answer it's ok to make an educated guess and plan the work accordingly.

Testimonials and references

Customers rarely ask for social proof, but they definitely want to see it if you've got it. Social proof is the reason why word of mouth is the best converting sales channel. When you're sold by someone who isn't being paid to do so, it reduces a lot of risk.

However, you shouldn't wait for notes of praise to poor in. You need to go out and ask for honest reviews from your past clients and colleagues.

Hours of availability

There's a lot of variability in how freelancers operate. Customers want to be sure you're there for them, especially if you're working remotely. Be clear about your availability, and provide details like timezone and out of hours etiquette.

It's worth knowing what your customer thinks of freelancers. Make sure you alleviate any issues they've had in the past, or think they might have with you. 50% of my customers had bad freelancer experiences, but finding that out meant I could serve them better.

Sales has a bad rap, because we conjure up images of men in poorly tailored suits on garage forecourts that won't leave you alone. The truth is, when you know what customers want, you barely have to sell to them directly. No-one cares about what you have to say anyway. They care about what you've done, who you've done it for and what you're going to do for them. Sales gets easier when you learn how to show customers what they want, and get out of the way.

Negotiation for freelancers

When most people think of negotiation, they think of hostages and they start to get nervous. But the negotiation phase is a good thing. It means your potential customer is very interested in your services. It's the last step in the sales process, matching their perceived value of what you do, to what they're willing to pay.

Before negotiations begin

What most freelancers fail to realise is that negotiation begins way before you're talking about prices.

Setting expectations from the start of the conversation and explaining your value properly lays the foundations for a good negotiation. If your client isn't aware of how valuable your solution is how can you expect them to pay fairly for it? Focus on getting good at explaining the value you're providing.

Base the price on the end result you're delivering to your client. Margins are relatively high when selling your services based on time, and it's easy to compare hourly prices to less experienced or less skilled peers, or even to themselves. Your client can justify paying for an end result easier than paying you a higher hourly rate than they get paid themselves. So frame your price around the project you're delivering (or better, the problem you're solving).

Remember that a good negotiation doesn't have one winner, ideally you're looking for a win-win situation. There is more value in a relationship built on mutual comfort, especially when it comes to repeat work. Get creative about how you can make a deal better for your client, without changing the price or reducing the scope of work. For example, I'm a big fan of offering warranties for digital services (incase things go wrong).

Work out the amount you're willing to walk away from, your minimum. And mentally prepare yourself to say no at anything lower. You can't afford to do business by losing money, unless you have no track record at all.

Let's negotiate

You should always be aiming to negotiate. Haggling on price means you're able to find the true value of your services to the customer. Which is why the age old advice of going in high still stands true. Starting with a higher price than either your or the client is comfortable with is a good sign, and it allows you both some room to figure out the true value. If you don't get pushback on price, you've basically left money behind — and that's bad for business.

The key to negotiating is not to do it with prices. The price is the price, you don't haggle at the supermarket do you? People don't haggle with lawyers, or architects. Ignore the common advice of not naming a price first. You should already know how much your time is worth to them. If you ask the client to name a price, 99% of the time the client will answer "Well, I don't know, you're the expert!". And they'd be right. Put the work in, to research and experiment with your pricing until you're confident with it.

If you're still experimenting with price, here's an easy formula I used to apply:

Take your cost price and double it. If you don't get challenged by your first customer, then double it again for the next. Keep doing it until you get some pushback. Now you've made room to figure out the sweet spot. At this point, don't back down, or suck in your teeth like a cliche mechanic. Change the conversation…

Negotiation isn't just about cost. If you need to reduce your price to fit a budget, work out a reduced scope of work to fit it. Negotiating on the amount of work involved keeps the integrity of your value in tact. If they don't have a budget but still insist on lowering the price, there is a strong chance that they're negotiating around risk, not price. Work on ways to reduce the risk, such as breaking the work up into milestones, or offering to work a trial period. Learn to spot the motives behind why a client negotiates and you'll be able to settle better mutual agreements.

If that fails, stop talking. Seriously, once you've named your price, stop selling. If a client asks for a lower price, try responding with, "That's lower than I'd like." and see what happens. Don't make suggestions, don't sell them on the work. Just be quiet and wait. This is the kind of thing you just have to try to see how powerful it can be in negotiating.

Finally, If you have a good reason to accommodate their reduction in price, you should have at least made some room in your margins to do so. Personally, I wouldn't compromise on price once I was confident with it. But there's always exceptions to the rule, such as wanting to work with this particular client, or the work that you do has a high chance of giving you more exposure/credentials.

In my experience, the freelancers that succeed are supremely confident in their pricing and are always prepared to walk away for anything less — so aim to get there. Holding onto these principals signals your value to clients and helps you grow a sustainable and respectable freelance business.

How to cold email a freelance lead

I've gotten to see a lot of client introduction emails over the past couple of months. I've realised that most freelancers don't know how to introduce themselves properly. There's really only one thing to say to a potential customer the first time - why do you want to work with them?

The goal

Sales aren't made in the first contact with a customer. They're teased out over a few interactions, where you learn as much as you can about them and their goals.

Your goal of an introduction email is to pass their bullshit filter. This means showing that you spent time getting to know who they are, and what they want. And why you're capable of delivering the results they're after. That's it. They don't need your life story, or your price list, or a detailed work proposal.

Why a cold email?

It's better than a cold call for a lot of reasons. But it is not a good way to sell. Make sure you learn who you're talking to, and using their name in the subject or header of your email. The first question you have to answer here is, "Is this email spam?". Personalisation will help you pass.

Find out what they do in the business and how their business works. Most of this can be learned through their website. If they have a blog, read it. Tell them what you like about their business, and why you want to work with them.

Portfolio

To a customer with a specific problem, a portfolio is not all relevant.

Send them a specific case study and tell them how it's relevant to them, what the results of that project were and why you think you can do the same for them. Bonus points if you can include that customer as a referee.

Give-away something

All businesses want a competitive edge. You can be theirs by showing you have insight into them and their industry. Such as, mentioning a recent change in regulations in their industry and asking their opinion on it. Or going through their website and suggesting any immediate improvements they could make. Obviously, don't be petty, make sure it's useful feedback. And be careful not to make assumptions about their business.

Call to action

Communicate with your client how they've asked to be communicated with. If you're leads are sourced online, this is going to be mostly by email. Don't insist on using other forms of communication because you prefer it.

Be specific about next steps, let them know your availability and suggest a day and time they can agree to immediately. Don't make them think, suggest a next step and make it easy to say "Yes".

Here's the kind of cold email I'd like to receive...

Hi Mitchell,
I came across your post looking for a copywriter and thought I would be a good fit. I like the biz model behind Workroll, much prefer it to commission based sites like UpWork.
I noticed you've already written a lot of content aimed at advanced freelancers. Have you thought about trying to convince people to become freelancers to begin with? A

lot of people are scared to make the leap, maybe we could help them?

I wrote a particular piece for smashing magazine about a year ago that you might like. It was "How to make your start-up first hire", and was aimed at start-ups.

I write content that is easy to understand, and helps increase engagement with customers. Most importantly for you, I'm very productive and can write 2 or 3 new pieces a day if required.

I'm free tomorrow at 2pm (BST) for a quick chat if you're around? My phone number is...

Thanks, Dave.

And don't forget to follow up!

Cold Calling for freelancers

Don't do it.

It's desperate, and it most cases annoying. If you have a good service and demonstrate it well enough, there are many better ways to generate leads. And they don't involve 300 rejections, and a maybe.

Client relationships are like real relationships. Would you ever cold call your way to a date?

Just in case, here are 5 solid reasons not to do it:
1. It's an unwelcome interruption for the customer
2. It's a great way to kill your motivation and your mood
3. You won't get to speak to the right person
4. You are going to hate it
5. The people you phone are going to hate it

The main reason I wouldn't cold call, is that it is very inefficient. It takes a lot of time to do right, and even then there is a 10% conversion just to get a follow up meeting/call. There are better ways to spend your time.

One sure fire way to win a freelance job

At the height of my own freelancing career I could boast a 10% conversion rate from first contact to closing the deal, this was up from 3% when I started. After years of optimising, the process of gathering leads to making contact and then winning the work, I discovered there was one tactic that I could rely on to give me an edge when competing with others to win work.

I originally got this idea from another industry, Architecture. When an architect sets out to build a big fancy new building they have to enter competitions and design the whole building before they've even been awarded the contract. At first this seems crazy, but there is so much competition out there for architects that the only alternative would be a race to the bottom in terms of the price the client would be willing to pay. At least this way, the winner gets paid a fair and good price for their services — because they won by being better for the client than the competition was.

Freemium

Remember that the biggest concern for a client looking for a freelancer is risk. Risk that you'll disappear, can't do what you say you can do, or can't turn their business goals into a solution that works for them. There is only one way I know to reduce that risk to practically zero — and that is to offer to work the first day, or first few days for free. If they decide they don't like what you're delivering. If they do like it and want to continue it's paid, just like the rest of the project.

Giving your clients an easy way to get rid of you is the same as giving them as easy way to say "Yes". The easier they can say yes, the better chance you have of working together in the long term. You can use the principal in the same way. For example: offering to travel to see them in their office for a kick off meeting. If the meeting is focused on getting started, you're almost guaranteed to walk away with the full project sold. It could be 1 page designed, or 1 article written — either way you're giving them a clue to what the future of the project would be like with you. And usually that's way more than the competition are willing to do.

I'm not advocating free or speculative work. I think of this more like a free trial, or money back guarantee. And when you do this, you must be sure that your chances of winning the full project are close to 100%, otherwise you're going to lose a lot of time.

Most freelancers shy away from giving anything away because of the horror stories we read about our peers being ripped off. Big agencies spew "No speculative work" like digital dogma. But the advice of big agencies is not going to be relevant to your freelance business. The reality is, trust is hard to build remotely and digitally. Sometimes it requires you to go back to basics and build that trust with people in person or as close to in person as possible.

When you're the one looking for work, you have to prove yourself before people will take a risk on you. If you have clients coming to you, then you've probably already done this, paid your dues and no longer need to build trust — because the trust is in your brand, and in the words of other people referring work to you.

How much should a freelancer charge?

Working out how much you cost is easy. But how much you should charge is a little more complex. There are many ways to charge for the work you do, but in my opinion there is only one way. If you want something more scalable than your average freelance business, you should charge for the value you created.

Cost

Work out how much you need a year, divide it by the number of hours you plan on working, with a buffer and 1 or 2 hours a day for sales and admin. Easy.

52 weeks - 4 weeks holiday - 2 weeks sick - 4 weeks buffer = 42 weeks

42 weeks = 210 days = 1260 hours (6 hour days)

$100k / 1140 hours = $90 an hour.

Don't go below this unless you can live on less. $100k is a great salary. Rarely do people start your freelance career there. But it is important to choose a salary you're comfortable with, covering all your expenses and making it worthwhile. Compare it to getting the perfect full-time job if you're stuck.

And remember, keep it to yourself. This is your cost, not your price.

Benefits of hourly rates

- Hourly rates are easy to work out. You can see what most other freelancers charge and you already know what your time costs.
- Customers expect to pay this way already.
- It can be a way to signal your experience and expertise. The higher the better. It can also be great for filtering for the best potential customers.

Downsides to hourly rates

- You will be compared on it, regardless of how fast you work or how good you are. This can be a problem for advanced freelancers.
- You are severely limited to how much you can earn. You're literally trading hours for money. So

good luck not feeling guilty when you're on holiday!

My opinion is, if your charging your customers by the hour, you're not a business, you're a temporary employee. Fixed prices are the way to go. You want to avoid charging for your time as much as possible. Fixed prices can be based on a rough estimate of time at first, then increased depending on rarity, value created and what the customer can afford. If something is hard to estimate, break it into smaller deliverables. That way you can scale what you do.

Fixed prices makes sense because the expectations are set upfront. The customer knows that they're getting and for how much. You know how much work is involved. Estimates need be rough, because they're impossible to get right.

Benefits of fixed pricing

- Your earnings can be more inline with the value you create, and you can concentrate on adding more value in less time.
- Your motivation will be to finish quickly and move onto the next piece of work. As long as

you keep your quality high, this shouldn't be a problem.
- You can fluctuate your price based on the tasks involved, whether you enjoy the work more, or what type of customer they are.

Downsides to fixed pricing

You might severely under-estimate the work involved and lose money. So adding a buffer is crucial.

What about the budget?

A budget is a necessity. This defines the scope of work involved. A common response to "What is your budget?", is "I don't know", or worse, "Not much". Well, you can buy a cheap car that goes slow, or an expensive car that goes faster. It's your job to tell the customer what kind of car they need. This means helping them decide a budget that gets them where they want to go.

Payment methods for freelancers

One of the most overlooked areas for freelancers is how they get paid. It's an important part of the experience from a customer's point of view, and you should go out of your way to make it as easy as possible.

Online

The common default for online payments is PayPal, so make sure you have it. It isn't ideal to use based on the horror stories out there about freezing account balances. But it is easily the most common way for freelancers to get paid online, mainly due to their bias towards protecting the customer. Your client will probably feel safer using PayPal if their fairly tech savvy.

Credit Cards

Probably one of the hardest ways to get paid, due to the amount of suspicion credit card payments come under, for the amount of fraud that takes place with them online. Stripe is a great way to protect yourself from consumer fraud, and hopefully adds a bit of reassurance to any client that knows about them. They make it super easy to set up payments online, but you will probably need to use a 3rd party to set up the form — check out their website for integrations.

Bank Transfer

Clients in the US will want to avoid bank transfers due to the high fees they incur. But bank transfer is one of the best ways to get paid as a freelancer, as there is no waiting period and usually no heavy fees from the receiver's point of view. The only issue you may run into is currency exchange rates, and that's why I'd recommend checking out TransferWise as their rates are superb and their experience from both sides of the transaction is pretty good, better than most banks.

Offline

With local clients you should be prepared and ok with accepting cash and cheques. After all, this is how most businesses operate and just because your a digital freelancer doesn't mean you should exclude these types of payment. They're a little more time consuming than every other way, but if that's what your client wants then you should accommodate them.

Incentives

The primary reason you're offering multiple ways to pay is to get paid quickly and efficiently. That's why I would also offer incentives for early payment, that you can build into your margins. For example, if your typical payment terms are 30 days, you're potentially losing out on 30 days of advertising budget to bring more work in. I used to offer a 10% discount for payment within 48 hours. Not everyone used it, but those that did, appreciated it.

Why bother? Because the faster you get paid the more you can spend on advertising or marketing and bring in work faster. Optimising how you get paid can make a big difference to your cash flow over the long term. And poor cash flow can kill a fledgling freelance business!

Ways you will not get paid for your work

Working with clients as a freelancer can be tricky. It's unlikely you'll actually meet any of your clients in person, but instead, you'll rely on an endless stream of emails and the odd phone or Skype call to talk through your latest project. There is definitely an element of trust that needs to be built up, and thankfully 9 times out of 10 you'll have a positive experience with your client.

But what happens if you don't get paid for your work? And is it ever fair to be asked for a discount on your proposed services?

This is quite possibly every freelancer's worst nightmare, so I've got some tips on what to look out for to prevent this from happening to you.

Being promised 'exposure' in return for your work

This can be a difficult one. If you're just starting out as a freelancer, you're in a quiet period waiting for work to come in, or wish to secure a new client, it can be really tempting to be lured into the promise of exposure if you agree to work for free. But how do we actually define 'exposure'? This could be through social media, being credited on a website, or earning a link back to your own website.

Don't fall for it. Whether you're offering a physical product, a service or your expertise, you need to be able to cover your costs - after all, time is money and you have to make a living. According to a survey conducted by the Association for Independent Professionals and the Freelancer Club, freelancers in creative industries lose around £5,394 every year through working for no pay. Unless the client is a charity you're close to or you're comfortable helping out an start-up company for example, always be open and honest, and ask for a fee. If your prospective client doesn't agree to this, walk away. It simply isn't worth your time.

Not receiving a clear brief

Like anything, you need to know what services are required from your client well in advance so that you can charge a fair price for your work. You might need to travel or you may need to do some additional out-of-hours editing. Knowing how many hours you need to put into the project requires a clear, well-structured brief with objectives and any additional resources required to help get the job done.

Now here's the tricky part. If your client doesn't provide this from the get-go, then realistically how are you expected to meet the objectives of the project? Before you start work on anything, ask your client to provide you with a detailed brief - the more information they include the better. And use it to create a contract before you begin any work. That way you'll protect yourself further on down the line.

It will help to create your own document that you can send to all clients before a project is agreed on and started. That way, you can ask for exactly what you need to start the work, and your client is less likely to change the goalposts by giving you a new brief; leaving you with additional work that will put you out of pocket. You also lessen the risk of your client being able to argue that you didn't fulfil their brief, as you will have everything documented in one handy place to protect yourself. As long as you can demonstrate that you met the objectives of the task, your client will have no choice but to pay you what you're owed.

It's also a great idea to have a list of key questions that you ask every client. The answers will always be different, but the questions will be relevant for every project and will enable your client to think about what they really want to achieve from your services. Feedback all of the collated information to the client before you begin, too. This will ensure you're both on the same page and will speed up the process.

Your client does a disappearing act

Now this is something I haven't personally had to face yet (thank goodness), but I do know of freelancers who have unfortunately had to deal with the stressful fall out from their client failing to reply to any emails or messages, and eventually becoming impossible to get hold of.

If this happens to you, the first thing to remember is not to panic. Difficult I know, but thankfully your rights are protected and there are routes you can go down to reclaim the money you're owed. I'd firstly suggest setting some dates for you to send out a polite reminder reminding them that payment is due. If you don't get a response from any of those, then try to call straight through to the person you've been dealing with. If this leads to a dead end, then it's time to get serious. If you're owed less than £10,000 then you can submit a claim to the Small Claims Court. You can also issue a Statutory Payment Demand, which gives the client 21 days to claim before you take the issue to Court. While this is certainly not ideal, sometimes the threat of Court action is enough to spring them into gear.

Unrealistic payment terms

Some businesses have company policies that set out payment terms of 90 days. That means you'll be waiting for payment for around 3 months, and you might not be in a position to be missing money for that long. This just isn't fair. Plus, if anything goes wrong with the finance team (i.e. you don't get paid), everyone's memory will suddenly become pretty hazy. Trust me - I've been there and it's not fun.

When setting out the terms for a new project, ask for a payment term of 7 days. There's absolutely no reason why a client can't arrange this for you, and if they can't then again, walk away. It's really not worth the headache further on down the line.

Another HUGE tip is to ask for a deposit beforehand of around 50% - especially if this client is new. You need time to build up that trust and while they may seem perfectly pleasant on email, when it comes to payment many people flake out.

Not getting work to clients on time

This one's pretty obvious, but we can't always blame the client for everything. Bottom line; if we don't meet deadlines or let the client know that work may be a little late (you should always ask if this is okay), then it's totally fair not to be paid. We enter into a contract the minute we begin work, and missing a deadline essentially breaches that agreement. Communication is key so if you need more time, be honest about it. Chances are your client will understand and allow you a short extension.

The bottom line

The most important tip I can give is to trust your gut. If something doesn't 'feel' right or if a client isn't being reasonable about your terms then it's best to walk away. While it's annoying to miss out on new work, it should be quality over quantity every time. Building up solid relationships with clients should be your number one goal, so focus on setting out your terms early on so you can continue strengthening the relationships you already have, and creating new ones that will last.

How freelancers can make sure they get paid

I can't understand why it happens, but it's common. Customers want work done fast, but won't extend the same urgency to getting you paid for it. Like with most issues in a client relationship, it can be alleviated by setting some expectations upfront. I think of this as creating a kind of social contract, one that people feel stronger about than a legal one. After all, not many of us have been sued, but most of us know what it feels like to break a personal commitment to someone.

I have a few tactics for avoiding non-payment, but even they won't stop it 100%. You'll encounter it one day, and it feels crap. But remember this is a business, and when it does happen, learn from the experience and identify how to stop it happening again.

Take a deposit

A deposit shows respect for your time and commitment. Paying for services in advance is rare but to me it makes complete sense. Generally 25–50% is an adequate commitment and will weed out anyone who is trying to pull a fast one. If your client can't pay a deposit, they probably don't have the budget to pay you in the first place. There are lots of excuses as to why a client can't pay a deposit but for me, it's non-negotiable.

Freelancer friendly terms

Insist on 7 day payment terms. Because there is really no reason to delay payment once a service has been delivered. Who cares if it's their company policy to pay after 90 days? It just isn't right and frankly I think it's a bit of a con.

Signing a standard supplier contract is vital, but I also implement an interest bearing non-payment clause to add a bit of urgency to the matter.

You also have legal options other than the courts, such as services that will follow up on your behalf, and even debt collection agencies. The key thing is to not worry too much about something that you don't have much control over — it's just unnecessary stress. Think about it happening, and prepare for it.

Milestones

Break your work up into milestones no longer than a month apart. Time based milestones for payment mean you will always be able to pay the bills. Nothing fucks a project up quicker than being distracted about how long it's going to take to get paid for it. Both you and your client will benefit from the focus that milestones give you.

Payment milestones can be, and should be in my opinion, separate from project milestones. Sometimes work can get extended or more complex outside of your control — and when that happens, you need the security of being paid to help you solve those problems effectively.

With enough experience you'll develop an instinct for the type of person that is like to flake on you, as the warning signs are quite obvious in hindsight. When you get that feeling again with a new client, don't hesitate to go with your gut.

Why advanced freelancers shouldn't use bidding websites

Freelance bidding websites attract a lot of freelance projects. They do this by encouraging competition and cheap prices. In this situation, nobody wins. The customer only gets what they paid for (not a lot). And the freelancer can't grow their business beyond the platform. To win a bid, you must compete on price. To lower your price, you must perform a basic service or reduce your costs. This goes against an advanced freelancers way of thinking. If you focus on adding as much value to a customers business as possible, everybody wins.

Services that produce results aren't basic. And can't be done on the cheap. They can, however, be constrained by a budget. That budget determines how much can be done towards improving an area of the customers business.

Bidding sites are useful for specific jobs, ones that are repetitive or thoughtless. If you want more leads for your dry cleaning business, buying an off-the-shelf website for $500 won't do it.

Problems for customers

It's easy for non-technical people to assume web services are cheap as standard. And they can be, if you do not care much about the customers real goals. But cheap solutions rarely deliver any value. If your aim is to provide the most possible value, you need to embed yourself in their business. And to win on that basis, you need to be clear about why they need, as a partner rather than a cheap product or service.

High-end customers want a trusted partner that can help them reach their goals, not a tool to try to do it themselves. Unless you know exactly what you need and you can spell it out very clearly, you're going to be left wanting.

Bidding sites do one thing very well, and that is to provide a guarantee that even if a project goes bad, the customer is always safe. But this can be emulated by offering the same kind of guarantees. For example, I've never seen a warranty offered for a web site — but why not?

Problems for freelancers

Where do I begin? A not so obvious problem is who owns the client relationship? They do of course. This is a problem for communication, trust, and longevity. Freelancers grow their business through great relationships with clients, not by completing to do lists.

Getting paid can be tricky. Sometimes the customer is not always right, regardless of what you may have heard. And I'm afraid you are a 2nd class citizen of the freelance bidding site due to the direction the money flows. They will always rule in favour of the customer, even if it's their fault.

Freelance bidding sites operate under a thin veil of being an independent arbitrator. Facilitating what looks like a free market, but is actually a race to the bottom. Like a free market, businesses pay a tax when they win a bid and make money. But unlike a free market, control is in the hands of the bidding site and their own interests.

Positives?

They are great for getting started though. If you don't need to earn much money, you can make some starting capital using these websites.

How to take advantage

So you didn't read this just to hear me rant about bidding sites, you came for a competitive edge right? Here are 2 things I would use them for:
1. Grab attention by bidding what you think the job is worth, rather than competing. Then put some real effort into a persuasive pitch, that draws out those customers looking for quality, not cheapness.
2. Analyse and copy the good parts of their marketing strategies, for your particular service or niche. For example, these sites are great at SEO and content marketing.

If you do nothing with them, you can at least revel in the thought that the services on offer are so basic, they will be done by computer AI in a few years. If you want to build a strong, sustainable freelance business, do things for your customers that make you hard to replace.

Why advanced freelancers shouldn't use contest websites

Speculative work (also known as spec. work, or contests) is a plague in the online creative industry. It damages how people outside the industry value the work we do. If it's your first introduction to freelance life, then it will stop you earning a good living and growing your freelance business.

What you'll earn

You'll get paid for around 5% of the work you do. That is, for every 20 projects you work on you have a good chance to get paid for 1 of them. You should note that the odds can fluctuate, depending on the freelancer. Some report their chances as low as 0.2%.

So you've done a minimum of 20 hours work, because you care about the quality of logos you produce right? And you've won 1 contest that pays you $300 — the average project price. Thats a measly $15 an hour earned. You'd need to complete 60 to 80 hours of work for $1,000 at this rate.

If your price is more than $15 per project (hint: it fucking should be!), this does not make economic sense.

If this still sounds like a lucrative opportunity, you should also know that contests are routinely abandoned. Also, your competition has a tendency to steal logos or icons, to improve their chances of winning.

Why you use them

Why do we fall for this exploitation? You're competing for short term, small gains when you could be building decent relationships with your clients. Why do they work? Well, they're designed to be addictive, just like gambling.

You'll spend an hour creating a few concepts for the chance to earn $300, that's great! Okay so it didn't work for the first time, but what's another hour? You're not too busy. Maybe you win one, wow what a feeling that would be! This is very typical of the strategies used to keep gamblers in casinos.

Contests are about pleasing the judges, giving them what they want. Freelancing is about working out what the clients goals are and helping them get there by making your own decisions. They hire you because you're supposed to have the answers. It not only cheapens the work we do, it doesn't build long lasting relationships that will help your freelance business grow.

8 red flags to avoid bad freelance clients

A bad client can cost you more than just the time spent dealing with the hassle they create. There are greater risks like not getting paid, or having legal issues. I have a strong gut feeling when dealing with a bad client, and every time I've ignored it, it ended badly. Over time I learned to recognise the things they did leading up to a bad break-up.

Demanding an urgent response

Emailing you at 11pm and getting angry at the lack of response usually means they haven't hired anyone before. This lack of experience will usually cascade into other areas of the project and cause further problems. Learn to manage your clients effectively, so they don't end up trying to manage you.

Make sure you're clear on what you're working hours are and stick to them, even if you're working late. Setting these boundaries is your job, if you don't do it you open yourself up to interpretation.

Asking for free or trial (unpaid) work

Very common, and obviously a bit dodgy. If someone doesn't value the work you do initially, why would they value it after that?

A common twist on this red flag is asking for quick changes, expecting them not to be billed.

The only time this is acceptable is if you have no track record at all. Otherwise you can reduce their risk with case studies and references.

Starting without a contract

A contract gives you a slightly higher than zero level of trust. But it's probably the most important thing you should do before starting work. My problem with contracts is being able to enforce them — it can cost more than it's worth. To me it's worth more psychologically.

Also, starting too fast or without them asking too many questions usually means they will try to push their luck. Loose boundaries allows unscrupulous clients to push the scope of their work without getting billed. If they legitimately want to start fast, they won't mind paying a rush fee for your trouble.

Complaining about cost

If they complain that the fee is too expensive for more than a couple of times, it probably means they aren't going to pay, or it's going to be difficult to get them to pay. Contracts are great for setting expectations and trust beforehand, but it costs money to enforce them. Don't trust your contract to make a bad client pay up. Instead, you can ask for a deposit, and have short milestones that allows you to be paid for your time before the work is completed.

A common way clients negotiate on price is to promise future work in exchange for a discount. This is a trap. You should only be charging for work they've promised you (in a contract). You aren't a credit agency. It isn't necessarily a red flag, they may just not have enough budget — but if that is the case, you can reduce the scope of work instead.

Lack of commitment

If the project isn't that important to them, it causes delays in signing off and paying their bills. That's why it's important to learn about them and their business before you work together. Find out what the project is for, how it will be used, and how important it is to them. If you're solving a painful problem, they're more likely to respect your boundaries, and appreciate the work you do.

Cutting corners

It might not seem obvious at first, but cutting corners is again, something that flows over into everything else the client may do. This can manifest as things such as, using Google images instead of buying stock. Clients that cut corners, will probably want a discount, and will probably ask for some things for free. Before you know it, you're losing money working for them. And the worst way this can manifest, is when they spot an opportunity to not pay for something, such as missing a deadline, they will jump on it.

Payment terms longer than 30 days

Poor cash flow kills businesses. You should aim to get paid within 7 days, and there really is no good reason not to be. If you're dealing with enterprise customers then you won't have a choice, but I would ask, what the fuck are you thinking working for those people? Enterprise or government customers are the worst. Leave them to the companies that like dealing with their particularly awful issues.

Unclear scope

If you're scope isn't clear, you're inviting scope creep in. It's possible to change scope completely, but make sure to settle up for the work finished and start again from the beginning. Any small changes should be clearly billed as extra. If your client complains about this and holds up your project, it's probably time to drop them.

This isn't such a strong red flag as the others, but if it happens repeatedly, you're probably losing money working with them over the long run.

The best tip for avoiding bad clients is to use your gut feeling. Most of the time this feeling is overridden by our greed, or desperation. But don't let it, it will hurt you later on. Aim to grow a sustainable freelance business, with good clients, and you'll enjoy every minute of working for them.

Working

How to handle these 6 types of freelance clients

There are so many client personalities it's hard to generalise them into just a few. But here I've noted the most common types that I came across and how I handled it.

"I'm not really sure what I want".

Don't expect clients to know what they want. You're the expert, so it's your job to figure that out. What you can expect them to know what problems they have that prompted them to talk to you. Spend as much time as possible getting to know what their problem is, where it comes from, and it impacts their business. You're trying to avoid starting down the wrong path, because when that happens, and project can turn into a complete waste of time for both parties.

An important step for any client project is to check-in on a daily basis (at least) with progress and ask for feedback. You'll avoid many problems by making the client a part of the process.

"I want to do it all, by tomorrow"

Pretty common with entrepreneurs. Although it can be funny the 20th time you've heard it, it's not a reason to scoff and tell them no. Its your job to turn their business goals into a manageable, pragmatic plan to get them where they're going. So the solution is simple — break their big dream down into milestones, with the most detail being in the first couple of weeks worth of work. Don't plan much further, because things will change.

If it's not acceptable to your customer, don't be offended. Just try to help them see why it has to be done that way and remember that most clients are talking to you because they don't know how things work themselves.

"I think you're worth it, but I can't afford it."

Very common, and easily solved. Be upfront and clear with your pricing. Is your rate fixed, hourly, daily e.t.c.? What happens if things go wrong? What happens if they change the work half way through? All these kind of pricing and payment problems should be figured out by you well before you approach any clients. If you don't know where to start, research all the options you have along with the pros and cons. the best way to figure out what works is to stick to one sales model and follow through with it — regardless of whether it works for you or not. If it doesn't work, you can change it for the next customer.

You might be in a position where you want or need the work, so a discount feels necessary. It rarely is. You can reduce the price of your service by reducing the scope of the project instead. Try and give them the most value possible for the budget they have. If you're really interested in helping them out, figure out ways they can do things for free or for themselves. It might not put money in your pocket, but if it can help them build a business then they may become a client in the future.

Swapping services can another be a good way to lower the prices for potential customers. If you do, make sure you're doing it for your own interests and it's something you would of paid for anyway — this is a business after all.

"…[silence]"

Sometimes a customer will not respond to email or voicemail regardless of how persistent you are. There really is no way to solve this other than to keep trying to get through to them. Most of the time it's due to illness or being away. Don't automatically assume they've ran off with your work or are trying to avoid you . Just give them time but keep following up. Running a business is more than a full-time job so small businesses generally need a bit more time to get their shit together.

Sometimes this can happen right after you issue an invoice, which is why it's important to set expectations when doing so. Make sure you have a short payment due date, because you can't afford to wait too long to get paid. 7 days is perfectly acceptable. If you still don't hear anything, that's when the interest charge clause in your contract kicks in, and it increases their bill the longer they wait. I've had this happen a couple of times and when I've reminded the client about it, they have suddenly cleared their schedule to talk to me and pay their bill. Both times this has happened to me I've cleared their interest charges, because the small amount of money means nothing if I've pissed off the customer for being strict. Remember it's just a deterrent — not a way to make more money.

"Can you try it like this...?"

This type of response usually follows on from a client that doesn't seem to know what they want. So the same kind of solution applies here — always make sure you have a clear idea of what success looks like to them. Ask as many questions as you can about what they're expecting. If you're trying to convince them to do it a certain way, be absolutely clear about what the results will be.

You can make sure that fixed priced projects have an end, by defining it as the amount of work done, not by them being happy with the results. It's important your clients are happy, but not at your expense. For example, when writing an article you can give a fixed price for 3 drafts and a finished piece, and then charge a small fee per additional draft. That way the project can run on and you're still getting paid.

If you can, find out if they've worked with freelancers before and if they have, try and get a reference about them from that freelancer. This can help you avoid or manage them better.

"No, that's not what I wanted."

It happens rarely, usually when I've been lazy about requirements gathering to begin with. The answer here is to recognise you've missed something. Go back to the beginning and ask them what they need. Make sure you get solid examples of what a successful outcome looks like to them.

Maybe you've been thorough and they still don't seem happy? If you can't figure out what's wrong it could be their fault — but to be honest I've only ever been paranoid that this is the case. It's never actually been true in all the time I've freelanced. Most of the time, going back over what they want and expect solves things.

The biggest challenge for freelancers is when you get a client that exhibits many of these traits at different times. At least when it does happen, even if it's not on this list, you know that there will be a solution, and it's just another problem to be solved.

Why customer service should be a freelancers priority

There are 2 main reasons I write so much about sales for freelancers. 1) Selling is depressing work for people who make things — because it's full of rejection. And 2) Freelancers are particularly bad at it. Even successful freelancers are constantly finding new customers, rather than leveraging their existing client base.

If you want to grow your freelance business, you should aim to stop outbound selling as soon as possible. The best way to do this is to keep the customers you've already sold to. Either by selling more, longer term services. Or by using their networks to earn more customers through them. This is why going beyond normal customer service is key to taming that magical sales channel successful freelancers go on about all the time: word of mouth.

It's cheaper, easier and faster

You've probably heard it already, that keeping an existing customer is cheaper than finding a new one. But it isn't just a cliche. For any business it's just good economics.

There's no question that it's easier to receive an inbound lead for a new project than go looking for it yourself. But it's also easier to deal with someone you already know, and faster to get legals and project planning in place before starting.

I won't spend too much energy explaining why inbound sales is better than outbound, it seems pretty obvious. So how do we start generating inbound lead? It's actually really easy, just not very common.

Think differently

For good customer service to translate to more work, it takes an extra level of thoughtfulness not found in most freelancers. It starts with the way you see the relationship. Are you there to do a bunch of jobs your client has asked for? Or are you there to solve the problem your client has, that prompted them to come up with their own solutions?

If you're designing a logo for a new store, did you think about how important this is going to be for their advertising? Once work is complete, did you go out of your way to explain how important a style guide would be, or maybe mock-up an example banner for their opening? Most business owners find it hard to juggle every responsibility they have. Helping them avoid their blind spots not only adds more value to their business, it turns you from a freelancer into a trusted partner. Instead of starting their search for a banner designer, you've already got it covered.

Part of good customer service isn't just solving problems in real time, it's identifying problems before they appear. This is the kind of customer service that turns into a real partnership between you and your client.

How a freelancer can provide exceptional customer service

It's clear that providing good customer service should be expected. But going beyond that can help your freelance business thrive. It can be easy to excel at this compared to most freelancers, by changing the way you think about your role.

Immerse yourself

You aren't there to throw up another generic landing page for a hot start-up. You're there to increase engagement, attract more visitors or increase conversion. Once you get out of the "do what I'm asked" mentality and into the "help do more" way of thinking, spotting ways to improve your service becomes simple.

Make sure the work you do aligns with the business goals. Understand how the business works, and why it exists. Buy their product. Talk to as many people inside the company as possible. Ask a lot of questions that begin with Why?

Set expectations

Be very clear about how you do things, why you do them that way and how much it will cost. People get angry when something isn't the way it should be in their head. You can avoid this by using your experience to recognise what information you should share up front. And once you're clear about how things should work, figure out what can go wrong. And when they do, be upfront about it. Setting good expectations is about being clear, and honest.

Exceed expectations

Once a client knows what to expect, it's easy to delight them by over-achieving. Finish projects early. Save them money. Deliver more. These are all things you can do easily. One way to get insight into what exceptional might mean to them, is to constantly ask for feedback, and make it part of the creation process. You don't have to take it all on board, but you should educate them as to why you're doing something differently.

Identify future problems

Running a business is hard. If you can, help out more. Freelancers are in a unique position to have seen many businesses operate in many industries. This gives you a broad (but shallow) perspective on what works and what doesn't. As long as you're not sharing trade secrets! The more value you add, the more you're worth to your client. This is the equivalent to reducing your costs, but in a positive way for both you and your customer.

Keep it personal

Whoever thinks business isn't personal, is a complete moron. Even though I much prefer doing things via email — most people appreciate a phone call or better, a visit in person. Especially to start things off, an in-person meeting can communicate much more than a bunch of emails ever can. Remember, most small businesses are intertwined with the owners life. When they're stressing you out or asking for more than they should of you, remember how much it means to them. I'm not saying everyone deserves this kind of help, but most people do.

Where should you work?

A big benefit of freelancing is the freedom to work wherever you want, whenever you want. No more 9-5, stuck in an office, only seeing the sunshine on weekends. But where you do want to work needs a little consideration to keep you happy, productive and making the most of your career. Expect a little trial and error to find your perfect fit, but there are some key things you can look out for on the way.

Working from home

The cheapest and most liberating of all the options. Living the dream. There are no additional costs on top of your usual monthly bills, which can be handy when starting out. You can work from your bed, from the bath, wherever the hell you like. No commute needed, which means extra time to spend on your work (or yourself! Bliss!). And working from home means you can be as flexible with your time as you like. Work can fit around kids and school, social life, whatever is important in your work/life balance.

As idyllic as it sounds, it does come with its downsides. Where are you going to work, a designated office space or the kitchen table? Will you have time where you won't be disturbed to get quality work done, or are you going to be fighting the chaos? Or on the opposite side of the scale, are you someone who lives for the office banter, who will be climbing the walls when faced with being on your own most of the time? The temptation to get other stuff done can be pretty powerful, especially when inspiration has deserted you and your hitting that brick wall. Spending 10 minutes watching TV can soon turn into a Netflix binge session. Even laundry can spiral out of control into a full spring clean when you aren't in a productive mood. Working from home is very doable, but make sure if you are a procrastinator or easily distracted you will need to go into this with your eyes open.

Office

Once you start making money, serious freelancers could find spending some on an office can be a good investment. Maybe you have just left office life and going back is your idea of hell, but you are working to your own rules, so relax.

An office would give you your own designated space, so you can work however you need to, to get the job done. Kick off your shoes, stick your inspiration all over the walls, or keep it your tidy space. Whatever you need to feel comfortable and productive. An office is also mentally a good way to get into the right frame of mind. Somewhere to concentrate on just the work without other distractions. And if you aren't having a productive day, then making yourself sit at your desk with nothing to do can help to focus you and keep you on task. It's also ideal if your work involves meeting with clients.

Shop around for the kind of office you need. Some are stand alone units, but others are serviced and this means you don't have to worry with separate bills for utilities and there is lots of flexibility in office size, and meeting spaces available to you. Some are run by local councils, and can offer additional guidance on areas of your business, or networking events for you to find new opportunities. The big issue with the office route is the cost. You need to have a steady income or a reserve of cash to pay for it, which when starting out can be tricky. Also check the paperwork carefully - be aware of 'hidden' costs such as leavers fees. And make sure it is easy to get to, if escaping the commute is your reason for freelancing. Make sure you check when the office is open. Some are only open during normal office hours, and if flexibility is one reason for going it alone then you need to look for something that suits - many offer 24hr access.

The most important thing to do is to be honest with yourself. Sometimes our ideal isn't what we would expect it to be, but there are ways to make all of these environments work for you.

What to do when you have no freelance work

It's normal to want to fill your schedule with paid client work. But when you're just working for clients you'll lose a lot of what makes you a good freelancer. Things like trying out new technologies or tactics. Taking time to work on things that give you pleasure or are useful for other people, like open source or education. There are a few things I'd recommend you do with time between projects, in-case you haven't thought of them already.

Opensource

We all use tools and information created by people in their spare time — now is a good opportunity to help out. This isn't just for tech freelancers either. Many projects could benefit from translation, copywriting, and even marketing.

Contributing isn't just altruistic, it can benefit your reputation and greatly increase the chances you'll be hired. By fixing issues or adding features, you're expanding the knowledge you have about that software. Showing that you not only work with the tools a client needs, but you contribute to the source of it, is the best way to de-risk a decision to hire you.

It can be daunting to get started, so I'd suggest researching it before you jump in. Here is a good place to start... https://opensource.guide/how-to-contribute/

Create digital goods

Do what you do for clients, but make it available to anyone. It's the scalable way to make money doing what you do. And if you're not interested in doing it for money, then you can give it away for free and earn a reputation for helping others.

Making digital products is an excellent way to expand your portfolio into industries or services that you want to work in. You can use the case study of creation, and sales to show how successful your work was.

Don't be fooled, it can take years to develop enough income for it to replace your freelance business. And the people who do this successful usually approach it as a full-time job itself. But it makes sense to fill your free time with things that contribute to growing your freelance business. One of the easiest marketplaces to get started on is Creative Market: https://creativemarket.com/sell

If you decide to sell your creations is too much hassle for not enough reward, you can always give them away for free. You'll be amazed at the attention you and your free resources will get from peers, and potential clients. And it comes with the added warm fuzzy feeling from seeing your work used by others. One way I used to enjoy giving back was contributing my photos to https://unsplash.com

Write

One of the best ways I know to reach as many interested people as possible is to write about what you've learned, and share what you know. Sharing the information with people in the same place as you is the easiest and quickest way to add value to the world. It comes with the added benefits of showcasing your knowledge to potential customers, or anyone that can help you grow your own business.

Putting your ideas out there is also the best way to formulate them, and receive criticism that can help you learn more. One way to validate your way of doing things, or your values, is to present them in front of people. Even if you don't think you have anything meaningful to say, try committing to a workshop or presentation of your ideas. That kind of commitment has a way of bringing out the best you have to offer.

Educate

Writing educational content is great for teaching yourself new things, as well as others. It can help you cement your own knowledge. When you learn something for the sake of your own work, you've probably realised that a lot of the theory is useless until it's applied. The application of your knowledge can also be achieved by trying to explain it to other people.

There are more upsides to educating others too. You can sell your content as a course and build an audience. Maybe even turn it into other kinds of gigs, like consulting or institutional education and training. There's also a lot of variety in the medium you can choose to share this kind of content, which keeps things interesting and fun.

Scheduling time for yourself is the most important thing for your skill set, and your moral. But there is one task you should be doing constantly — building relationships with potential business partners or clients. Always be available to talk about new projects or help people flesh out their ideas, and generally make yourself useful to others. Because if you do, you'll always have incoming work, and time to work on your own things.

Holidays for freelancers

Between negotiating your rate, chasing up unpaid invoices and answering emails at 11 pm on a Friday - at some point in your freelance career, you'll wonder about taking a holiday.

Holidays are a very different situation when you're a freelancer. You have neither a co-worker for your out of office, nor the perk of paid annual leave. Any vacation you take will chip a hole into your finances, and may even cost you a client.

So, can you take a holiday? Whether you're a seasoned freelancer looking to take your first longer holiday, or you're new to the game, here are some steps to prepare for your trip.

Examine your finances

The employed are paid for any time spent on the beach. They can order a second bottle of wine and book an impromptu jet-skiing excursion - it doesn't matter if they chew through their holiday budget because a paycheque is waiting back at home.

As a freelancer - any time that you are not working, you are not earning. Perhaps this is why one out of four freelancers in the UK don't take a holiday.

As you plan your holiday, examine your finances with a fine-toothed comb. Are you on top of all outgoings - rent, bills, etc? Commit to a daily budget for your trip. Note down all expenses including insurance, injections and suncream.

Send all invoices for completed work promptly, so payments don't go astray. The bane of freelance life is overdue payment for your services, so allow time for chasing. Will you have work waiting for you as soon as you return from holiday to jump back into, or will you come back and need to hustle?

Prepare your clients for your holiday.

Besides the temporary loss of income, you will fret over the impact your holiday might have on your relationships with clients. All freelancers fear their expendability; what if you are replaced?

Losing a client is a risk when you're away. Building that on-going working relationship is a challenge. If you have been collaborating for a while and have a rapport, your client will probably retain your services once you return. Clarify deadlines and deliver early to allow time for any amends.

Be transparent - give clients plenty of notice before your holiday and communicate exactly what you can and cannot deliver.

Consider any issues that might arise while you're away. If you're in business support, do your clients have all the log-ins they will need? Is the software you're developing likely to be presented to an investor while you're away?

Use a platform such as Airtable to get everything in order.

You could arrange for another freelancer within the same industry as cover, particularly for a long trip. A network of freelancers in your field of expertise is a valuable tool - so make connections and form a trusted pool, whether via co-working spaces or online communities.

Establish a communication protocol

You need to unwind on holiday. However, as a freelancer, it is more likely that any work woes will follow you to your destination, and you may prefer to stay connected. There is debate over checking emails while on holiday, but you will need to make the call on exactly how close an eye you keep on your inbox.

Good practice is to agree a set time every day or two when you check in and respond to messages from clients. You can request that clients should only contact you if the work is urgent, it pays to be assertive and set this boundary.

Do prepare for flexibility - you're on holiday, and you need a degree of spontaneity. Do not feel guilty about any time you are uncontactable, but communicate when it is the case.

New and prospective clients

If you have recently begun working with a new client who you are keen to keep on your books, again, transparency is key. Tell them early that you have a holiday in the pipeline. Shooting over an email as you buckle your seatbelt on the plane will ring alarm bells about whether they can trust you.

Use the time before your holiday to truly shine - give your client a reason to remember you. Add a little extra value to your pilot project, or deliver earlier than they requested.

In case a prospective client reaches out, indicate on your bounceback that you will be checking emails at set times of the day. You might not be able to respond to their query in full, but at least you can send them an acknowledgement and that you'll be in touch once home.

Travelling and working

If you work remotely, it might be tempting to think you could put aside a few hours a day to keep on top of things. This could be an option for a longer trip. Bear in mind practicalities like interference from a new time zone and patchy Wi-fi. You need to allow yourself to be spontaneous and let your holiday surprise you. Those two hours a day will probably escalate.

Digital nomads travel and work, but they stay in one place for a longer time and have routines, including using co-working spaces. A short holiday is different. You have a limited time at your destination, you'll want to squeeze in as much as possible.

Do carry a notebook and jot down any ideas that might strike while travelling. 'Going on vacation provides a wealth of novelty to spur creativity,' writes behavioural scientist Jon Levy.

Should you book that flight?

If you don't give yourself time to unplug and recharge your batteries, then you won't function at full capacity. Everyone needs a break, says Dr Jenny Leeser of BUPA, to protect our mental health. You might put yourself at greater risk of losing work if your standards slip.

Experts confirm that taking a rest has important benefits which include improved mental power, greater well-being and are at less risk of burnout.

Remember, everyone is human - clients will understand.

Budgeting for freelancers

Working as an independent professional can be quite challenging and demanding, especially when it comes to managing finances. Most self-employed professionals often freelance and, as a result, they tend to have unpredictable incomes. With inconsistent income, it is often too hard for freelancers to budget for the different cycles of their jobs.

Admittedly, budgeting for the valley seasons and saving for long term needs, such as kid's school fees and retirement can be quite daunting for freelancers. Although it's not easy, it is achievable

While successful budgeting requires a steady income and careful planning, freelancers lack a steady income. But, even with the erratic income, they can use the following tips to budget for both short-term and long-term needs.

To begin, a budget is simply a way of ascertaining how much money you require to meet your daily needs and prioritising things to ensure that you don't exceed the amount. Irrespective of your situation, a budget is an essential part of ensuring that your finances are sustainable.

If you are a freelancer, a consultant, a commissioned salesperson, a temp worker, or any other worker with fluctuating incomes, a budget is of utmost importance.

Know Your Baseline

Whether you are a full-time employee or freelancer, the underlying money principle is that you should never spend more than you earn. Consequently, you need to know how you spend your money for you to budget efficiently.

For those who have a steady income, budgeting will generally entail allocating spending categories to your limit of income. Some freelancers have enough consistent gigs that they can use them to create their budgets and leave out any one-offs for their debts and savings account.

However, for most freelancers and other independent professionals, the process entails working backwards. You have to start with the money you spend to determine how much you need. Simply stated, for freelancers, their expenditures must be stable because their incomes are unstable.

So, if you don't have an existing budget, start by tracking your spending. What do you spend your money on mostly? List these items on a notebook or spreadsheet. How much do you spend on these items? You can start by focusing on your monthly recurring expenses, such as housing, groceries, transportation, utilities etc. You can then use your old credit and debit card statements to ascertain your average monthly discretionary spending on thing such as eating out, shopping, travel, etc.

According to the 50/20/30 rule, expenditures fall into three categories: essentials, priorities and lifestyle. From the rule, financial experts advise that freelancers should strive to live on 50 per cent of their income with the other half shared between flexible expenses and savings -30 per cent and 20 per cent respectively. Staying within this guideline will enable you to meet your long term financial objectives, regardless of your income amount.

Using the guideline, your baseline expenditures are those that fall under the essentials category-the ones that you can't do without and are incurred every month. So, focus on estimating the costs of the following:

1. Groceries

Plan your baseline expenditure by focusing on the lowest food cost that suits your circumstances. Your grocery expenditures shouldn't include a lot of extras, such as coffee shops, wine, fast food hope, etc.

If you intend to minimise on your food cost, take that into account when drawing up your budget, but try to be realistic with your cost estimates. You can decide to track your spending for a few weeks to assist you in getting the best estimates for your monthly expenditure.

Preferably, you can learn to only shop once a week, based on the meals you've already planned. Moreover, you can team up with fellow freelancers and friends to buy in bulk from large retail outlets.

2. Housing and Utilities

For most people, mortgage or rent form part of the essential expenses in the home. If you are fortunate to be staying in a house that you don't pay rent, include your minimum monthly housing cost in your baseline. Ensure that your property tax bills and homeowners insurance are accurately captured in your total.

If you are staying in a region which requires air-conditioning and heating as necessities, include the monthly bills for the same costs in your baseline. However, if you come from areas with moderate regions, utility bills are categorised under the lifestyle expenditures which don't constitute the baseline expenditures.

If you work from home, account for your phone and internet costs because they are a necessity and constitute a part of the baseline expenditures.

3. Medical Costs

A key reason why most people file for bankruptcy is because of medical bills, so it is crucial for freelancers to have a medical cover. Include the cost of medical insurance in your baseline estimates and any other outstanding medical expenditure.

When looking for a medical insurance plan, learn the habit of negotiating and comparison shopping, whenever possible. Shop around and get advice from other freelancers before choosing a particular insurance cover to give you the best payout options that will suit our lifestyle.

4. Transportation

Determine whether you need to use transportation to work and consider the lowest cost of transport available for your job. If you have your own car, factor in the auto insurance, car loan repayments, gas expenses, garaging costs and maintenance costs. If you use Uber or some taxi services regularly, factor in the cost estimates and include them in your budget. Try to be realistic with your cost estimates and sum up the costs you'll incur on transportation per month to include it in your baseline estimates.

If you can manage to bring down the essential expense to less than 50 per cent of your income, you'll have more money to allocate to your savings and discretionary spending. So, in the end, you may find yourself tweaking the rule to 45/25/30 or whatever it may be.
However, it is noteworthy that the rule doesn't work for everyone. If you are a parent with young children, you will incur a lot of money on necessities, and you may be operating at 60/20/20. However, once you are done with childcare, you may revert to 50/20/30 or anything close. Nonetheless, the 50/20/30 is only a guideline.

Determine Your Income Target

Once you've determined your monthly baseline expenditure, you can now figure out the pay you will write to yourself every month. Using an online tax calculator, determine how much tax you will pay the government and add the numbers to your baseline budget.

Alternatively, you can hire a tax expert who specialises in freelancers and independent contractors to help you get your tax obligations right. Once you've added the tax to your baseline budget, the figure you arrive at is your bare minimum monthly income requirement.

Anything you get above the bare income requirement should go to your financial priorities first, and then cater for your emergency savings, and any remainder will be for your lifestyle expenditures.

Set Up Different Bank Accounts

Because you have essentials, priorities and lifestyle expenditures, and you need to spend in all the categories, you will, therefore, need to set up separate bank accounts.

1. Business account

Here, you will have all your cheques auto-deposited and all invoice payments from clients deposited on time. For your daily cash, you may have to rely on tips, if you get any. From the business account, you should only make three transfers per month to the below-listed accounts.

2. Personal Account

This account caters for all your bills- lifestyle, priorities and essentials. The rule of thumb is that you should not spend more than you've allocated yourself for the month. If you have performed very well and your income has exceeded your target, and you have money that you can spend on your savings, this account receives any bonus that you may wish to allocate yourself.

3. Emergency Savings

Each month, after paying yourself for your baseline needs and transferred money for your priority needed, you should deposit money into an emergency fund. Freelancers should always aim to channel at least six months of net income to their emergency savings account to insulate them from the following situations:

- Loss of job and you have bills such as rent and living expenses
- A medical emergency
- A car breakdown, specifically if it is your primary means of transport to work
- Emergency home expenses, such as a leaking roof, AVC breakdown, etc.
- Bereavement-related expenses

4. Priority Savings

The priority savings account holds money for your semiannual and annual payments, such as home insurance, property taxes and income taxes. Additionally, the account is the repository for money intended for specific vital goals, such as college savings for a child, mortgage down payment, and student loans repayments.

Keeping your finances healthy takes self-control, commitment, and consistency. If you use the strategies above, you have a much better chance of meeting your budget goals.

Growing

Turn your freelance project into a long-term client

The key to building a sustainable freelance business is turning short-term projects into long term customers. You do this by being consistently good at what you do and building trust between you and the client. You can build trust by not just doing what you're paid to do, but going beyond that and becoming a partner. So what's the difference between a hired gun and a partner?

Adding more value

It's easy to fall into the trap of just doing what you're told to get paid. But it's a losing strategy over the long term. You should be embedding yourself in the client's business to identify other problems you can solve and see them before they arise. You're most likely being hired as a specialist in an area the client knows very little about, so you're perfectly placed to save them from potential pitfalls or issues that may arise. And you should be doing this for free. Whether or not your customer wants to pay you to solve that problem, you're building trust.

However, there is an element of timing to how you do this. Remember to concentrate on the project at hand, but take notes so that once it's finished you can then bring up other areas that may need your attention. Do not try to sell more services when you haven't even finished the work you were hired to do in the first place!

Follow up

It's your job to follow up and check-in with how things are going after a project has ended. They may be having issues with the work you left them with, in which case it's in your best interest to help them with it. But it can also be useful to keep in touch with a business as it grows, as they will likely need your help again in the future.

Having a more vested interest in a client's business shows that you're more committed and loyal than most freelancers. And makes you a good choice to rehire in the future. Most successful freelancers know the value of actually caring about their previous customers, because it results in more word of mouth referrals and repeat business to the point where they no longer go out and look for work anymore.

If you take a longer term approach to helping your clients, you'll be well on your way to building a more sustainable freelance business.

Stand out from the crowd on job sites

Job sites are a popular way for freelancers to find work, but a quick glance at any of them will show you just what a crowded marketplace it is.

To have any hope of landing work without the dreaded 'race to the bottom', you need an edge.

Think of a job site as being a bit like a speed-dating agency. First impressions count. To stand out from the crowd, you need to hit the ground running and then pick up the pace even more.

There are several things you can do to boost your chances of standing out on job sites.

Polish Your Profile

You may think the first thing potential clients notice is your job proposal, and often you'll be right. But there's a good chance they'll check out your profile for a quick glimpse of you before they decide to spend any time reading your proposal.

The more responses they've had to job adverts, the more likely they'll use profiles to create an initial shortlist.

In your profile:
Highlight achievements before education. Clients don't care if you have three degrees and a PhD, but they do care that you can do the job. Showing them previous work in a similar area is the best demonstration of your expertise.
Use Clear language. Say what you can do clearly and simply. It's tempting to use big words and lots of jargon but avoid it. If you're not sure whether you're using jargon, imagine you're explaining it to your mother. Will she understand the 'insider' terms you're using?
Take pride in your accomplishments. No need to brag, but don't be too modest either. If you've increased sales by 30%, say so. If you've extended circulation by half a million, quote the numbers. Be as specific as you can.

Learn from people higher up the chain by looking at the top profiles in your industry or sector. How are the high flyers presenting themselves? Can you make similar claims?

Remember, the words, tone and style you choose for your profile will reflect your brand, your personality and style. The style of your profile should mirror the market you wish to attract.

Target Your Proposals

Sending in fewer, more carefully targeted proposals will help you stand out from the crowd
It is very important to make the offers you do send as personal as possible and address the client's request directly. The more specific you can be, the more they will know you are genuinely interested in helping them out.

Know Your Skill Level

When you're searching for suitable clients on job sites, search within your skill set.

While a bit of stretching is necessary for growth, offering to do jobs you know little about is stressful. Working beyond your current level could also mean your work doesn't quite make the grade, especially when you are starting out.

Quote a Suitable Price

You'll find a range of prices and budgets for similar jobs. Just about all advice on setting your pay rate starts the same: decide how much you need to survive then work out your hourly or fixed rate for specific tasks.

It's sound advice but, on job sites, there's a caveat: You have to take into account the potential client's stated budget.

Wherever you can, align your fee with the amount offered. You can (and should) negotiate a little if you have a strong argument but, when you're trying to attract attention, you'll stand out more if your offer fits in with the client's request.

Don't be tempted to undercut either - the client may wonder what they aren't getting from you that the other freelancers can provide.

Build Your Reputation

Your reputation on job sites can make or break your chances of finding work. You build your reputation by earning good feedback for a job well done. Most job sites offer star ratings, and these can let clients filter out lower rated freelancers.

Like book reviews, your feedback from previous clients influences how potential new clients will regard working with you.

To earn your five-star rating:

Deliver what you promise.
Meet deadlines.
Over-deliver if possible – over-delivering means providing something extra that adds value the client wasn't expecting.
Update clients on progress.
Ask for information if you need it.
Stay positive, professional and polite.

Telling your client you want to provide a top-rated service is a subtle way of letting them know you want a five-star review.

Competition is fierce in the freelance world, but there is plenty of work for those who stand out from the crowd. It's not too hard to raise your head above the others when you know your market and follow a few basic guidelines.

How delegating tasks can improve your workflow

Delegating tasks will not only improve your workflow, but this simple act can also save you money in the long term. They say you have to speculate to accumulate, as a freelancer this idiom couldn't be more accurate. Trying to keep all the balls in the air as an independent contractor can at times be daunting, and overwhelming. This is especially true if you are struggling to perform tasks you aren't moderately skilled in; the more time you spend trying to come to terms with areas outside of your expertise, more valuable earning time is significantly lost. Hiring a professional to do these jobs for you guarantees a job well done, and will give you peace of mind.

Who should you call on for help? The business world is made up of a plethora of professional bodies who will take your work to market. Below are some examples of how hiring-in can support your growing business.

Accounts

As a sole trader with few overheads and minimal expenses, self-assessment seems pretty straightforward. As your business starts to grow and you find yourself delegating tasks, it becomes more important to understand what you are entitled to – especially if you work from home – and the different types of expenses you can claim. HMRC are very helpful in this respect, but they don't want you to know about some of the hidden claims you are entitled to. An accountant might seem like yet another unnecessary expense, but as their fee comes out of what they get back for you from the taxman, it is money well spent.

Website design

In this modern world of technology, your website is the window to your business. Although there are many 'self-builds' out there, they still take up a lot of your valuable time, and by the time you've paid for all the add-ons, you may as well have paid a professional in the first instance. The majority of people browse on smartphones and tablets, getting your site to perform well, and behave on these mediums is key in keeping them on your pages. So much time can be wasted dealing with annoying little glitches a professional will iron out in seconds. Starter packages can be as little as £100, and you generally have ongoing support and back up to deal with the inevitable problems that pop up from time to time.

Administration

Self-discipline is the most important trait in a freelancer, especially if you are working from home. However, some people find the organisation of running a business doesn't come naturally. Staring at a full email inbox, booking appointments, conducting research, writing letters, all take up valuable time and cost you money. You can carry on with the tasks you are skilled in by getting someone else to manage these daily, or weekly, activities for you. It doesn't need to cost as much as you might think. There are plenty of freelance virtual assistants out there who will be happy to do as little or as much work you need. No salary to pay, just on an 'as and when' basis when you need extra help.

Marketing

We all have our individual strengths and skills. You can be a highly successful entrepreneur, but have no idea how to market yourself. If you don't keep up with current trends, you aren't going to be bringing in the business. Hiring a marketing expert will save you time and earn you money as they use their in-depth knowledge to get you and/or your business out there. There is no shortage of social media experts to generate a valuable following to spread the word on what it is you do. Social media has become one of the biggest and most successful, marketing strategies in recent years. For this to work for you, it takes dedication and commitment, when your time could be better spent on other things. Again, hiring a marketing expert need not break the bank; once you are set up and running, they will post engaging content on a regular basis, and you can pay for work done as you go along.

Copywriting

Writing copy is a skill born of years of experience in the industry. Your website designer won't be doing this task for you. Every piece of text will go straight up on the site without being checked by them for errors. That isn't their job. Their skill is in the design. There is nothing worse for a business than to have a website full of grammatical errors, spelling mistakes, and punctuation omissions. This shows a lack of professionalism, which will not encourage people to stay on your site and engage with you. Skimping on copy will not save you money, neither will it make you money. If you know this is an area of weakness, then outsource it, or you may as well not have a website at all.

Proofreading and editing

It can be hard when you are close to something, and understand the subject matter, to be objective to the flow of writing, accessibility to the reader, or to spot glaring errors. There is a variety of software to help with checking your content, but after all, they are only robots and can't adjust to the tone of voice you are writing in. It takes an expert in the field to realise when the corrections are necessary, or when Grammarly doesn't understand your target audience. It takes a trained eye, a human eye, to see what you can't see, and correct it for you.

Take a fresh look at all the tasks you are doing. Is it your area of expertise or could someone do it better? Is it taking up valuable time, where you could make more money than you would be paying someone else to do it? Fortunately, there are plenty of sites you can find a freelancer to do any of the above jobs and many more.

Give it a try and see how beneficial it can be to your workflow.

6 ways to optimise sales conversion for freelancer

After being rejected a few times, you start to wonder what you're doing wrong. Well, maybe it's nothing and you just haven't gotten lucky yet. But most probably it's because you're doing it wrong. There are so many ways for a sale to die, that you need to apply every trick in the book to keep it alive.

Follow up until you get a "No."

Before I used to follow up, my conversion rate from initial contact to a closed deal was something like 1 in 30. Afterwards it was closer to 1 in 10. It made the biggest difference to my freelance sales by far.

Talk

Email is a horrible way to have a conversation and share ideas. Go through proposals on the phone or in person. A back and forth chat between 2 or more people is where the magic happens. You'll find out more about your customer and their project in less time, and they'll be more invested in you.

References and testimonials

People buy in herds. The more sales you have for a particular niche, the more sales you'll get. Show this by asking customers to write short testimonials. Showing that you know how to achieve other people's goals will give your potential customers a lot of confidence in you.

Relevant experience

It's really difficult to imagine how creative work will turn out before it's been done. You need to help your customer with this by showing work samples and telling stories about what you've done that has worked in the past. If you don't have the relevant experience or examples, you need to get some. You can do this for free with a non-profit organisation, or you can make up a fictional client and do the work for them.

Business insight

Just because you're hired to write copy or design a logo, doesn't mean you can't offer your advice in other areas of their business. Building a business is hard. You know that and your customers are experiencing it too. Help people out as much as you can and you'll be amazed how much it comes back to you.

After sales

Word of mouth beats any sales channel, ever. Follow up with your customers after the work is completed to remind them to recommend you. Offer incentives even. Another term for this could be "Influencer marketing", because anyone can be an influencer in the right situation. So turn your customers into your best marketing tool by teaching them how to recommend you to their friends and colleagues.

Give something away

Often the best way to remove risk for a customer, and get your foot in the door, is to give your time and expertise for free. To avoid being screwed over you can do things that benefit you in other ways. For example, a usability review of their website is a great way to show your insight, but can also be published to attract more potential customers.

How to win freelance work without proposals

Writing proposals has to be the most time consuming and least motivating part of freelance work. A lot of effort goes into the production and presentation, making sure all the clients questions are answered as well as having answers for any questions that might come up in the future. There is a trick to delivering proposals that doesn't require the typical production values, although you still have to write them.

The problem with delivering a proposal is no matter how great a writer you are, it's still a very impersonal way to start a working relationship. By accident, I discovered a trick that changed the way I saw writing proposals and ultimately won me more work. It also had the added benefit of not tying me into a specific project scope, and invited more collaboration from the client.

I still had to write them, but it would be in a more casual, note form. At its core a proposal is a roadmap for the services you're carrying out, how you are going to do it and why.

It should start with your understanding of the project, what problem you're trying to solve and what success looks like. From there we should get into the details of how the work will be carried out, including milestones, timeframes and cost. A lot of effort goes into how to display this information so that it's easy to understand. This highlights the 2nd problem with written proposals, making sure they're understood.

Once we're done with the project specifics, let the client know what the next step is. Except, the next step for the client is to close your proposal and get back to their other work. And that's the 3rd problem I have with emailing proposals. Most proposal deliveries require a follow up just to remind the client that you're ready to get started.

Do it in person

Not rocket science is it? Write your proposal and then phone your client or meet them in person to go through it with them. The benefits of doing it this way are numerous.

- Making sure you understand their project and it fits in with their business

- Optimising how they want the work carried out, in real time
- Making sure they understand the value in your solution
- Making sure they understand the costs and timeframes
- Carry out your next steps instantly, such as negotiation on price and start date
- Building rapport with the person you're going to be working with

When you start delivering your proposals in person, you'll quickly realise how ridiculously impersonal it was to deliver written proposals. You can get things started much faster in person by covering much more ground and making sure everyone has the same understanding of the project. What used to take half a day to a day can now be done in half the time.

Rejection

What if they're not convinced by your in person pitch? Or maybe they're just cautious about saying yes in person or on the phone, without thinking it through further. You can still follow up with a written proposal, based on how well you think it went in person. At this point you'll have a good idea whether or not it's worth the extra effort.

How client testimonials will help

Client testimonials are important for any freelancer, especially if you primarily operate online. Testimonials give freelancers authenticity and allow potential customers to see the experience others have had with them.

What are client testimonials?

Testimonials are statements that highlight the experience a satisfied customer has had with a business, including freelancers. Testimonials can be used as a marketing tool on your website or corresponding social media platforms.

Why are testimonials important in winning work?

Testimonials give you credibility, show real examples of your expertise and reassure customers that you can provide what you are offering. Testimonials can also strengthen your personal brand as they are a portfolio of experiences from satisfied customers.

Word Steam references how testimonials are a way for potential customers to relate to you through a customer similar to them. They see experiences from an actual customer, not a paid sponsorship or a paid influencer. Ultimately, testimonials are a way for you to build trust between yourself and potential clients.

Once you have built a foundation of trust between yourself and your clients, the likelihood of them wanting to work with you will increase. Due to advancements in technology, the number of touchpoints involved in a customer's journey has increased. Websites are an example of this. When a client is researching you, it will improve the credibility of what you are offering if you have testimonials on your website.

How to get testimonials from past and current clients
Asking for a testimonial can seem awkward, but only if you do not know the process. You can't just expect clients to come to you with their testimonials; you have to be proactive in asking.

When do you ask for a testimonial?

The worst thing you could do when asking for a testimonial is to ask before you have started any work. You should ask your customers to provide a testimonial after the work has been done. If the work is ongoing, you can ask for a testimonial once the customer has started getting value from working with you.

Asking for a testimonial

There are several ways you can ask for a testimonial. You can ask for a testimonial during a client meeting if you have an established relationship with the client. You should not make the entire meeting about the testimonial it should be brought up naturally when your client shows they are pleased with your work.
The best way to ask for a testimonial is through an email. If you have a face-to-face dialogue with your customers, you can mention that you would like them to provide a testimonial.

What to include when asking

When requesting a testimonial through an email, remember to include the following elements:
Be polite and make it personal
Proof of experience – Get them to write their experience
Provide a deadline
Examples of previous testimonials

Ask to use their first and last name. If privacy is an issue ask to use their first name and the initial of the last name Photo of the client, while this is not mandatory, it adds to the authenticity of the post

Don't keep asking. Your client might be reluctant to ask if you are pestering them for a testimonial. Once you have asked for a testimonial, leave it up to the customer to respond. Do not risk turning positive customer experience into a negative one.

There is nothing worse than receiving an email with a greeting such as 'hello customer'. Incorporate a personal yet formal approach to your email. Do not beat around the bush; share with them the purpose of the email. For example, 'Can you write a testimonial about the experience you have had while you were working with me, that I can add to my testimonial page please?'

Forbes highlights how it might be hard for customers to write a testimonial; therefore, by providing examples you take the stress away. Customers will also be less likely to procrastinate if examples are given. To prevent further procrastination also give some form of a deadline for the testimonial. For example, 'Preferable, I would love to have the testimonial before the end of the work week, thank you'.

When you receive the testimonial, make sure you thank them for their time and for writing the testimonial.

Short, Direct, Authentic.

No one wants to read through a wall of text. Therefore, short testimonials will be more effective as they are more likely to be read. If your client gives you a long testimonial, you can take sentences out for your website or social media platforms. Just make sure your client is aware of any changes you make to their testimonial.

Forms of testimonials

Many definitions of testimonials refer to it as a written statement; however, video testimonials are just as effective, if not more. Video testimonials are especially effective if you have social media platforms connected to your business. According to CompuKol Communications, a video testimonial can 'touch people emotionally and visually'; which means customers will connect with the brand on a personal level.

On social media platforms, videos are also more likely to be shared, which means your business will reach a wider audience.

Using testimonials

The most beneficial aspect about testimonials is that, once you have permission off of the client, you can use them as much or as little as you want.

Many businesses have testimonial pages on their website. While this is a good idea to have all your testimonials in one place, it might not be the best way to use them. Testimonials that discuss certain products or services can be placed next to the product or service it references.

Testimonials can be used on social media, for example, on Twitter you can share the testimonial with the hashtag #testimonialtuesday. This will improve your credibility and show your expertise in your sector.

Along with your website and social media platforms you can put testimonials on your blog, brochures, press releases, email campaigns and more.

Next steps

Every freelancer should have a collection of testimonials to show the experience others have had with them. Using the tips mentioned, at the end of your next project, ask your client for a testimonial.

How you can double your freelance income overnight

Double your hourly rate. Seriously. Okay there's a bit more to it, but that's the gist of it.

The art of pricing your services correctly is something that takes experience and experimentation to get right. I have 2 methods for increasing your freelance rate:

Get uncomfortable

When you're starting out, most freelancers have the common sense to work out their costs and then price themselves slightly higher than that, because, you know, business. This is a fine way to get started as long as you don't plan on growing your freelance business in the future. And if you're not growing, you're dying.

The approach you should take to pricing is that you don't know what it should be, and when you don't know something, you should experiment. My advice is to start with your minimum and double it. If that's a price that makes you uncomfortable, that's a good sign. If not, double it again. Accept your first client project and pitch your services at that price. If it's an easy sale, don't congratulate yourself just yet. You just fucked up. A 100% conversion rate or lack of negotiation means you severely undervalued your services. But that's okay, that's why we're experimenting, right?

For your next client project, double your prices again. Feeling embarrassed? Good. Your aiming for the client to give you some pushback to signal that you're close to a potential sweet spot with pricing. It's okay if they laugh at you. The price of something should make you slightly uncomfortable, but willing to pay for it anyway — that's where the real profit lies. Aim to negotiate on every sale.

Once you've got some pushback, the next time you're pitching your services you should put a bit more effort and learning into the pre-negotiation sales. Learn to express the value of your solution so well that when it comes to negotiate again, it's easier or it's non-existent. Then we're back to step 1, double your prices again. You're now in a constant cycle of improvement of either your selling ability or negotiation skills — and the only thing to come out of that will be more profit and easier sales. This will teach you to identify the motives for your client to hire you and how best to solve their problems for them. This is at the core of being a successful freelancer.

You're aim is to get to a point where you feel like you've exhausted your pre-negotiation sales skills (N.B. you haven't) and negotiation is always tough but the sale happens anyway. Sales should be difficult so don't shy away from it, it's part of your job as a freelancer.

Maximise sales

It's pretty obvious, but most freelancers don't do it. Identify problems your client has in other areas and offer to fix them too. Get good at identifying problems before they happen, or finding new ways to grow their business for them and offer solutions.

Freelancers are notorious for just doing as they're told and nothing more. You can actually improve the perception of yourself by being more than just a job list ticker. Integrate yourself into your client's business and help them make more money to share with you!

You can also sell more whilst alleviating risks for your clients, such as ongoing support or some form of warranty for the work you've done. As long as you're focused on providing value for your client and not just squeezing them for more money, your intentions will come across well and will help increase your project success rates and hopefully result in more repeat work.

www.ingramcontent.com/pod-product-compliance
Lightning Source LLC
Chambersburg PA
CBHW071455220526
45472CB00003B/813